D1549386

The Air Pilot's
WEATHER GUIDE

The Air Pilot's
WEATHER
GUIDE

Ingrid Holford

Airlife
England.

Front Cover:
Primary (inner) and Secondary (outer) rainbow, seen by a photographer standing with his back to the sun and looking towards a shower of rain. Rainbows are nearly always seen on vigorous convection days when there is frequent alternation of sunshine and showers. *The Aviation Picture Library.*

Printed in England by Livesey Ltd., Shrewsbury.

Airlife Publishing Ltd.

7 St. John's Hill, Shrewsbury, England.

Contents

Introduction and acknowledgements

This book is written for all those who take to the air, whether powered by engine or wind alone, or even free falling. It presents the basic facts of meteorology so that aviators may understand professional forecasts and the limits of their accuracy, and take appropriate avoiding action when predictions go wrong, as sometimes happens. Meteorology is an inexact science and there are very few mathematical answers possible.

The book is dedicated to the many aviators who have fed back factual evidence about the invisible wind, and thereby helped meteorologists understand their difficult subject.

The term aviators includes women as well as men, and for the purposes of this book *he* and *him* include *she* and *her*, because if I had to write both all the time you would be as frustrated with the text as you often are with the weather!

I would like to thank all the pilots who have allowed me to quiz them on flying matters, in particular Air Vice-Marshal Wilfrid Oulton, who kindly read the whole script and made constructive suggestions.

My thanks also to the production staff of Airlife Publishing Ltd who have been so helpful in converting my ideas into the final book; and thanks also to those who have contributed photographs, acknowledgements for which are given under each picture which is not my own. Chapter 12 was originally written for the monthly journal, *Pilots International*.

1 Sunshine and Heat

It is ironical that the bad weather which frequently curtails flying is created initially by sunshine, which is too often elusive at ground level.

The Sun radiates electromagnetic waves, rather less than half of which reach Earth where they are reflected or absorbed according to the surfaces they strike. Rough surfaces absorb more energy than smooth ones, which are good reflectors; dark colours have better absorption qualities than light colours. The energy which is absorbed becomes heat and raises the temperature of the surface concerned, but there is an unfair distribution

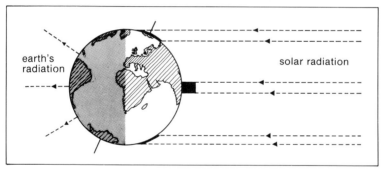

earth's radiation

solar radiation

Each hemisphere experiences seasons according to whether it tilts towards or away from the Sun, which is so far away that its rays are as good as parallel when they reach Earth. They provide more heat when concentrated over a small area from overhead than when they strike the Earth obliquely.

around our world. The Sun is so far away that its rays reach Earth in parallel beams, but those which strike from overhead concentrate heat benefits over a smaller area than those which strike obliquely and are spread over a wider area. The Sun raises temperatures far more at the Equator than at the Poles and the areas between are composed of complicated sea and land surfaces which warm at different rates. Weather is the means by which nature attempts to redress the inequalities of heat within our atmosphere.

Heat is a restless commodity, always on the move from a hot to a colder material by conduction, re-radiation or convection, and this results in an extremely complicated pattern of surface temperatures around the world.

Water warms slowly but is a good conductor of heat, spreading it quickly throughout the volume concerned. Hence the temperature of the sea surface, which is what affects weather, hardly rises at all from one day to another and only gradually to a maximum after a whole summer season. Water also conducts heat quickly away from an immersed human body, and ditching in the sea, specially in the colder months, can have fatal consequences.

Air, on the other hand, is a poor conductor of heat which makes it a good insulator. In order to retain body heat in cold weather or when flying in open cockpits, one needs several layers of cellular clothing, having plenty of air pockets for heat retention, as well as a top layer of wind-cheating impervious material.

Land temperatures are affected by these different conductive properties of air and water. Soil consists of millions of particles of rock which warm quickly in sunshine. When soil is dry, the air pockets separating the rock particles insulate heat from seeping downwards into the soil and nearly all the heat is used to boost the temperature at the surface. When soil is wet, however, water assists heat to spread over a greater depth of soil and then surface temperature only rises a little. Grass, which is mainly water, warms evenly and slowly in sunshine but dry sand can get so hot that it burns the soles of one's feet.

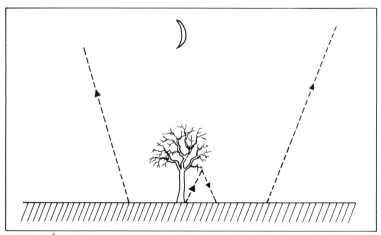

Cloudless skies permit the loss of heat away from Earth into the higher atmosphere.

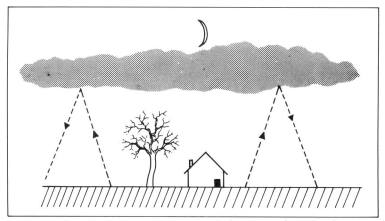

Cloud acts as a blanket and restricts heat loss from the Earth.

Heat is re-radiated again from all surfaces on Earth, always from a hot to a colder substance. When sunbathing on the beach you get benefit from direct radiation from the Sun and also from re-radiation off the sand; your own body then re-radiates heat, a ceaseless give-and-take which has little effect upon weather when the all-powerful Sun shines by day.

After dark, however, it's a different matter. The Earth is the principal radiator of heat, which escapes into space unless there is some intervening blanket of cloud to absorb or reflect it back towards the ground. On a cloudless night the overhanging eaves of a house or even bare branches of a tree prevent some heat loss. Surfaces which warm easily in sunshine lose heat just as easily at night.

The surface of water also re-radiates heat and the consequent fall in temperature results in a change of character in the fluid. The cooler surface layer becomes more dense and sinks, allowing warmer water from below to well upwards and get cooled in turn. This continuous up and down movement, called *upside-down convection*, means that the sea surface temperature hardly changes at all in any one night and only gradually to a minimum at the end of a whole winter season.

The important fact, as far as weather is concerned, is that however much the temperature of land fluctuates during any 24-hour period, the temperature of the sea surface remains virtually the same. Sometimes higher than the temperature of the land, sometimes lower. Rivers and estuaries, being shallower, change temperature more than deep water but less than dry land.

The temperature of air, the medium in which aviators fly and

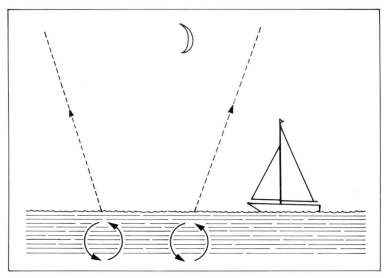

Radiation of heat from a water surface leads to upside-down convection within the water.

weather forms, is determined at second hand; not directly by the Sun's rays but by contact with surfaces on Earth. Air warms near the ground and temperature generally cools with height. Within the 6-10 miles of atmosphere closest to Earth, called the troposphere, one is more likely to get frozen than frizzled.

Air is fluid and therefore able to move around like water. A thin layer of air resting on a warmer surface acquires heat by

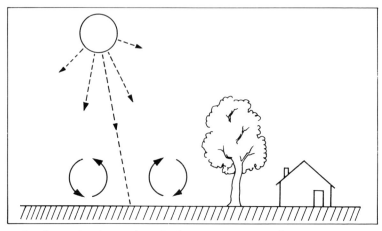

Land warming in sunshine leads to convection in air.

conduction and its temperature rises. This makes it less dense so that it rises and makes room on the warming surface for colder and denser air from alongside or above. Little by little air warms and circulates by this process called *convection*, to raise air temperature in a room, garden or town, even when the Sun is not directly shining.

Warm air is lighter than cold, a principle used to good advantage by balloonists. *M. J. Hammersley*

Air cools when it lies in contact with any surface colder than itself, perhaps the ground cooling by re-radiation on still, cloudless nights, or very cold sea or a snow surface. As temperature falls air gets more dense and settles on to flat ground to get still further cooled, while the air above may remain temporarily much warmer. This is called an *inversion* of temperature and accounts for the fact that fruit blossom may avoid damage on some nights even if temperature at ground level is well below freezing. Similarly, smoke lies in a horizontal pall above a bonfire on still, cloudless nights because it cannot rise above the lid of warmer air above.

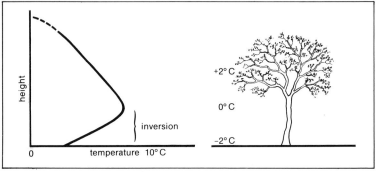

An inversion of temperature exists when air becomes warmer with increasing height above ground.

An inversion often keeps fruit blossom safe even when there is frost on the ground

If air cools over sloping ground then it slides downhill under gravity, to form a down-slope wind, similar to the little wind blowing on to one's feet on opening a refrigerator door. Wind is simply moving air, initiated because of differences in air temperature and density. A simple principle, endlessly complicated by the huge scale of world weather.

Food for Thought
Why does the Sun raise ground temperatures more at the Equator than at the Poles?
When is sea temperature at its maximum?
Which ground surfaces heat best in sunshine?
Why does the temperature of the sea surface change so little in any one night?
How does warmth circulate through the lower atmosphere?
On what kind of nights would you expect a temperature inversion near the ground?
What is wind?

2 Earth's Atmosphere

The Earth spins within an envelope of gases, which can be roughly divided into five categories according to the temperature characteristics of the atmosphere. The troposphere lies closest to the Earth, up to about 7 miles high over the Poles and about 10 miles above the Equator, within which air temperature generally decreases with height. Above, the Stratosphere, up to about 30 miles above the Earth, has constant or increasing temperature; beyond that the Mesosphere, up to 55 miles high registers decreasing temperature with height. Within the next two bands, the Thermosphere and the Exosphere, temperature increases to decidedly uncomfortable levels. Each of these layers is separated by a narrow band in which the temperature gradient changes gear, so to speak. The Tropopause divides Troposphere from Stratosphere, and the Stratopause and Mesopause indicate the limits of the other layers. Weather forms within the Troposphere and, for the purposes of this book, the term atmosphere will be used to describe this layer only.

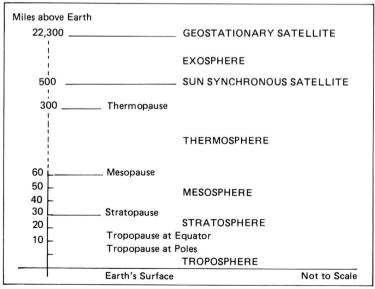

Indication of the relatively shallow Troposphere, in which weather forms.

The atmosphere consists of a mixture of gases in fixed proportion, mainly 78% nitrogen and 21% oxygen, together with the invisible gas water vapour in variable amounts. Torricelli discovered in 1643 that the atmosphere has weight and exerts a pressure, which can be measured by the balancing column of mercury in a tube evacuated of air. The atmospheric pressure varies every day, usually between 29 and 31 inches of mercury. The modern unit is the millibar (sometimes called hectopascal after the scientist Blaise Pascal) where 1000 millibars is equivalent to the pressure of 29.53 inches of mercury at 0°C. The various gases exert pressure independently, nitrogen about 750mb at the surface of the Earth, oxygen about 230mb. Water vapour pressure may be as little as 0.2mb when air temperature is -40°C and can hold little vapour, or as much as 42.4mb when air temperature is 30°C and saturated with vapour. Pressure generally varies between 990 and 1040mb, according to weather, and occasionally is much more or much less. In normal living conditions at ground level nobody notices this pressure or its daily variations because air presses inward and outward on all surfaces including our bodies. Curious, when you think that the weight of the atmosphere over each square yard of Earth is getting on for 10 tons!

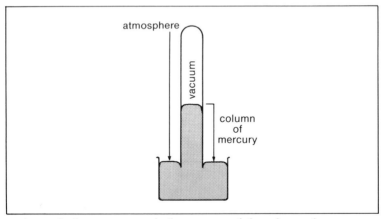

Atmospheric pressure equals the pressure of the column of mercury.

Atmospheric pressure decreases with altitude because the higher you go the less the column of air overhead. Pressure is less on the roof of a block of flats than in the foyer, less on a hill top than in the valley and of course much less when flying than on the airfield below. The human body acclimatises itself easily to pressure change when walking up a hill or even such mountains as we have in the British Isles. Climbing anything as high as Mount Everest, however, calls for gradual acclimatisation at various stages together with oxygen to reinforce the diminished supply at high altitude. People who live up in the Andes have developed barrel chests and a quick breathing system to deal with the problem of rarified atmosphere.

Oxygen is necessary for an alert mind, and is absorbed by the blood according to the atmospheric pressure prevailing. Ascending rapidly into the upper air therefore creates problems for the aviator. At 10,000 ft some oxygen may be needed to overcome loss of efficiency and mental ability; at 20,000 ft a supply of oxygen is necessary to remain conscious. Around 40,000 ft there is not enough atmospheric pressure to force even a full supply of oxygen into the blood and pressurised suits or cabins are essential. People adapt differently to their surroundings and James Glaisher, meteorologist and balloonist, who was one of the first to explore the upper atmosphere, recorded 29,000 ft on 5 September 1862 before he became unconscious.

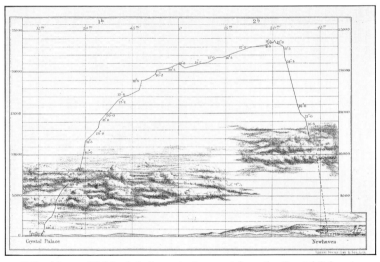

Path of James Glaisher's balloon, in its ascent from the Crystal Palace to New Haven, 18 April 1863, showing how temperature decreased with height above ground. From *Travels in the Air* by James Glaisher.

His pilot, Coxwell, was so paralysed that he could only just open the control valve with his teeth and thus saved both their lives. They were lucky to have survived at a time when the altitude risk was not fully appreciated.

The rate of pressure decrease with altitude is about 1 mb for every 30 feet ascent, up to about 20,000 ft. Thereafter the rate is more like 50 feet for every millibar pressure of the rarefied atmosphere. These figures vary according to air temperature, because cold air is heavier than warm. The depth of each succeeding 100 mb layer of atmosphere increases with altitude, ie, a greater thickness of atmosphere is needed to exert the same pressure.

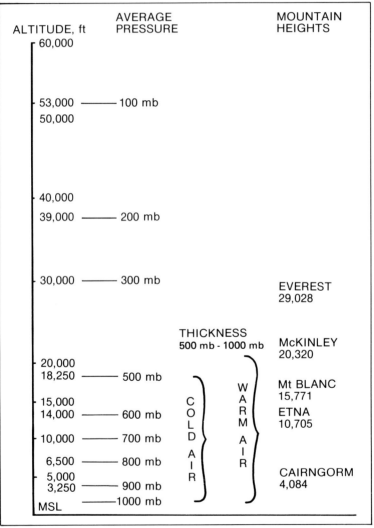

Atmospheric pressure decreases with height, and at about 18,000 ft is approximately half that at sea level. The height of the 500 mb level is lower in cold air than in warm. Mountain heights for comparison.

At 18,000 ft atmospheric pressure is approximately half that at sea level. When air is specially cold aloft, the thickness of the layer of air between 1000 mb and 500 mb is less than it would be if the air were warmer and less dense. In other words, the height of the 500 mb pressure level is lower in cold air than when warm air is seeping aloft into the area. Meteorologists use maps showing the height of the 500 mb pressure level and the thickness of the 1000 mb-500 mb layer when preparing forecasts. They are less important to aviators than the concept of pressure at Mean Sea Level.

Weather and atmospheric pressure are related, but only if the pressure variation due solely to the height above sea level is eliminated. The ground must be metaphorically ironed flat by adding to every pressure reading made on high ground the pressure of an imaginary column of air, the same height as the barometer is above sea level. Mean Sea Level (MSL) pressure is therefore always an estimate, unless actually recorded on a small boat or on the shore. Meteorologists take into account the temperature and density of air when correcting to MSL.

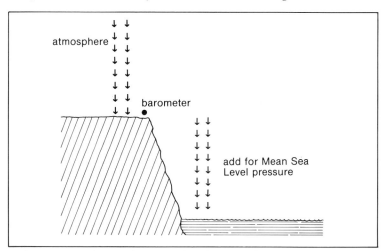

Pressure provides significant weather clues only if corrected to Mean Sea Level (MSL)

The aneroid barometer was invented in 1843 and soon replaced mercury instruments, which are very susceptible to damage, for everyday use. The aneroid consists of several corrugated capsules, partially evacuated of air, which compress or expand under variations in atmospheric pressure. A pointer is connected to a dial face carrying a circular scale. A second, movable pointer is fixed to the dial and set above the pressure value read at any one time, so that one can note rise or fall when the barometer is read the next time.

A barograph is a barometer whose movements are traced, by stylus or pen, on a chart wrapped around a rotating drum. This gives a record of pressure movement, called 'tendency'.

Standard aneroid barograph, showing typical alterations of atmospheric pressure during two weeks. Barographs adapted for gliding purposes record for a matter of several hours rather than several days, have a linkage to ensure a vertical scale of height, and should be properly compensated for use at very low temperatures.

An altimeter is an aneroid barometer adapted to record height above ground or sea level. Pressure is inversely related to altitude, so that the greater the altitude the lower is the pressure recorded. Likewise, a barograph can be used as a recording altimeter, and when set and sealed provides a permanent trace of flight in gliding competitions.

The snag with using a barometer as an altimeter is obvious. Atmospheric pressure changes every day, whereas the ground or sea below is always the same. There can be no fixed line of reference on the altimeter, only one which is re-set, by means of screw and subscale, before each flight to take account of the prevailing atmospheric pressure.

There are four principal settings for the altimeter subscale, values for which can be obtained from the local weather office or from traffic control.

Combined standby altimeter and airspeed indicator, suitable for commercial aircraft. Altimeter setting 1013 (QNE) or 29.92 inches mercury. The pointer revolves once for every thousand feet while the counter clocks up thousands and tens of thousands of feet. Illustration shows 2740 ft. *Smiths Industries*

Miniature altimeter, suitable for pocket or hanging round the neck, recording by pointer in tens of metres, up to 5 km registering in window beneath zero marked on the face. *Thommen*

QFE is the atmospheric pressure on the airfield, and when set into the subscale causes the altimeter to read zero when the plane is on the ground or height above airfield when flying. It follows, therefore, that when the plane is already on the ground, the pilot can twiddle the screw of the subscale until the altimeter reads zero, and the subscale will automatically register QFE without any need to refer to the weather office.

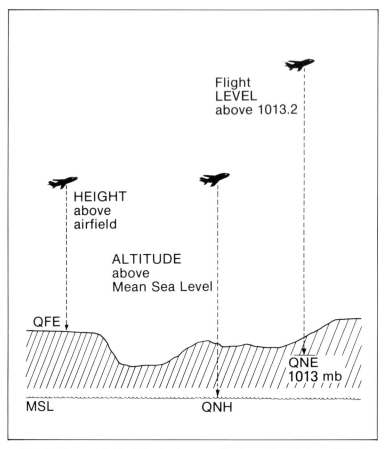

Height above airfield, Altitude above sea level, and Level above 1013.2 mb with altimeter settings of QFE, QNH, QNE respectively.

QNH is the estimated MSL pressure, which when entered into the subscale causes the altimeter to register the height of the airfield above MSL (AMSL) when the plane is on the ground or the altitude AMSL when flying. For aviation purposes, QNH is a simple addition to airfield pressure (QFE) of 1 mb for every 30 ft above sea level, without corrections for air temperature. Pilots must allow for a possible error of ± minus 50 ft in altimeter reading.

This setting, too, can be made without reference to the weather office if the aircraft is already on the ground and the airfield height AMSL is known. Turn the subscale screw until the altimeter reads the known airfield height and the subscale will automatically register MSL pressure.

QNH Regional is the QNH value adjusted for probable variations over a specific region and period of time to take account of forecast weather. It may give a lower-than-true reading on the altimeter for safety sake, and *must* be obtained from the weather office because it may not give the real height of the airfield when the plane is on the ground.

QNE is a subscale setting of 1013.2 mb, used for flight levels well above any dangerous high ground so that all aircraft fly with their altimeters similarly adjusted. This apparently inconsequential value of pressure is the International Standard Atmosphere, at specified temperature and density, by which all instruments are calibrated.
Note that specific words are used when communicating about subscale settings, in order to avoid possible confusion.
HEIGHT above airfield is used with a QFE setting
ALTITUDE above sea level when flying with QNH setting
LEVEL when flying on a 1013.2 mb setting.

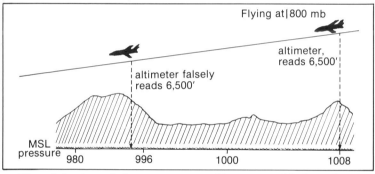

When flying towards low pressure, an altimeter may falsely read too high.

Food for thought
What is the tropopause?
How does temperature vary with height within the troposphere?
What is the difference between a millibar and a hectopascal?
How does atmospheric pressure change with altitude?
At what altitude does lack of oxygen start to create problems for aviators?
What is the approximate atmospheric pressure at 18,000 ft?
What correction is made to barometer readings in order to make them significant for weather?
Why must one re-set an altimeter before each flight?
With which altimeter settings are the words height, altitude and level used exclusively?

3 Pressure Winds

As far as weather is concerned, actual values of atmospheric pressure at any particular place are less significant than the differences between one place and another. Barometer readings, corrected to MSL, are plotted on to maps in the location they were made and contour maps of pressure drawn which are comparable to geographical contour maps of height. These pressure contour maps tell tales about the wind.

Isobars are lines joining places having equal atmospheric pressure at the same moment of time. Each line is a closed circuit around a centre of high or low pressure, and no line crosses any other — that would give an impossible two values for one place.

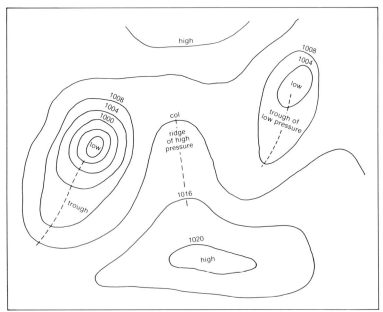

Typical fluid pattern of isobars, showing pressure gradient.

The isobars together create pressure patterns and show pressure gradient in the same way that geographical contours delineate heights around peaks and valleys. Atmospheric pressure generally changes smoothly from one place to another so that, within limits, a meteorologist can interpolate or extrapolate from a few known pressures to ascertain others. This makes it possible to draw isobars for whole values of MSL pressure, either side of 1000 mb, as a standard practice, the intervals dependent upon the scale of the map. A map of the British Isles only can accommodate isobars drawn at two, even one, millibar intervals; the small maps published in the daily newspapers, covering the Atlantic and western Europe can only take isobars at 8 mb spacing.

The pressure gradient is the rate of pressure change across the isobars, analogous to the gradient of a hill. The closer the isobars, the steeper the gradient.

Wind is moving air, which tries to flow from a region of high pressure to one of low. However, it only achieves this on the small scale, for instance draughts under a door or zephyrs off cool grass on to a hot tarmac runway. On a global scale, the jigsaw of warm and cold surfaces, land and sea, between Poles and Equator complicates movements of air enormously. For one thing, there is a geostrophic force due to the Earth's rotation which deflects air to the right in the Northern Hemisphere and to the left in the Southern. For another, there are vertical winds altering the temperature of air throughout the whole depth of the atmosphere. It would be a nightmare to determine wind speed and direction from all these contradictory temperature factors, but for the fact that the Dutch scientist Buys Ballot discovered in 1857 a simple connection between pressure and wind.

Buys Ballot's Law states that at 2000 ft above ground, assumed to be free from the drag of surface friction, wind in the Northern Hemisphere blows parallel to the isobars so that low pressure is on the left hand when there is a following wind. In other words, wind blows anti-clockwise around low pressure and clockwise round high.

However, the Southern Hemisphere really is upside-down to the Northern, even though rotating in the same direction about a common axis. So there the wind rule is reversed — low pressure is on the right hand with a following wind, and wind blows clockwise around low pressure, anticlockwise around high.

Surface wind, close to ground or sea, suffers drag from friction and manages to follow the high-to-low direction a little better. It differs from the 2000 ft wind by about 30° over land and by about 10° over smooth sea, always converging towards lowest pressure in depression or cyclone, and diverging from highest in an anticylone, in both hemispheres. Wind is said to **back** when it changes direction in a counterclockwise manner, and to **veer** when it changes in a clockwise manner.

Wind speed at 2000 ft is inversely proportional to the distance between the isobars. The closer together the lines, the stronger the speed which can be determined by placing a graduated scale, appropriate to the map being used, at right angles across the isobars. Surface wind is about ⅓ the speed of wind at 2000 ft over rough ground and about ⅔ over calm sea. However, this is a rather unrealistic concept because turbulence creates frequent fluctuations in direction and speed near the ground as the wind encounters obstacles in its path. Wind may gust to a speed equal to that at 2000 ft one minute and then lull to almost nothing, even in gales.

Winds at higher altitudes generally become stronger with height all the way to the tropopause and the direction becomes more westerly. There are nearly always head winds when flying from Europe to America near the tropopause and tail winds on the return. Wind speed is often more than 100 kts near the tropopause, sometimes 200 kts in jet streams, which are cores of high speed wind embedded within slower winds. Jet streams become stronger in winter when there is greater contrast between polar and equatorial air temperatures.

Wind rules are more difficult to convey by words than to 'see' by studying the charts themselves. Look at the examples given and hold a finger anywhere above the righthand side of the page, to represent an airfield. Then move the page below the finger and notice how the pressure changes as the weather advances towards the airfield. Play the game again by holding the page still but moving the finger above the charts in any direction to represent a powered aircraft, flying faster than the weather advances, and note again how pressure values change en route, how the wind changes direction and how the altimeter reading may be affected. An aircraft flying towards low pressure will experience starboard drift in the Northern Hemisphere and port drift in the Southern.

Upper air charts, similar to those drawn for MSL pressure, can be made using atmospheric pressure at any specified height above ground — 10,000 ft, 20,000 ft etc. Wind at those levels can be measured from the isobars in just the same way that wind at 2000 ft is determined from the MSL isobars.

However, it is more practical for meteorologists to measure the altitudes of a constant pressure value, say 500 mb or 700 mb and then plot contour lines of height. These produce similar

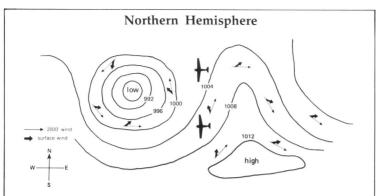

Northern Hemisphere

The closer the isobars the stronger the wind. 2000 ft wind blows parallel to the isobars, anticlockwise round low pressure, clockwise round high.

Surface wind is backed from that at 2000 ft, converging towards low pressure, diverging from high.

When flying towards low pressure and north of centre, wind changes by backing and gives starboard drift.

When flying towards low pressure and south of centre, wind changes by veering and gives starboard drift.

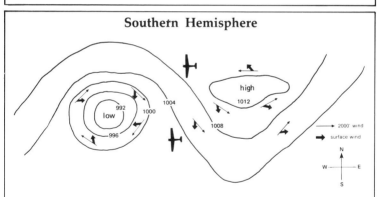

Southern Hemisphere

The closer the isobars, the stronger the wind. 2000 ft wind blows parallel to the isobars, clockwise round low pressure, anticlockwise round high.

Surface wind is veered from that at 2000 ft, converging towards low pressure, diverging from high.

When flying towards low pressure and north of centre, wind changes by backing and gives port drift.

When flying towards low pressure and south of centre, wind changes by veering and gives port drift.

patterns to the constant altitude charts and reflect the features of the surface pressure charts, but in modified manner. The patterns have a wider sweep, there are fewer closed circulations and the centres are usually displaced sideways from those below. But the wind at the constant pressure level follows the same rules that it does at 2000 ft; parallel to the contours so that the lowest height is on the left in the Northern Hemisphere with a following wind, and on the right in the Southern Hemisphere. The closer together the contour lines, the stronger the wind.

Balance within the atmosphere is achieved by means of large scale vertical movements of air, which complement the horizontal pressure patterns. Air rises in huge convection clouds over *equatorial latitudes*, where MSL pressure is fairly uniform and on the low side, around 1013 mb.

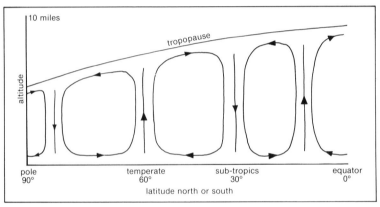

The balance of Earth's atmosphere is achieved by huge vertical cellular movements

At the tropopause air spills over above the *sub-tropical high pressure* belt and subsides to replace diverging air near the ground. There is little cloud in the sub-tropics, which contain many dry deserts.

In the *temperate latitudes,* winds diverging from the subtropical highs and polar highs meet and conflict. Cold air undercuts warm, to create lift, cloud and rain in the travelling low pressure circulations called depressions. Bad weather alternates with short periods of high pressure extending in ridges from either north or south. Occasionally, ridges develop into high pressure circulations, called anticyclones, to give heat waves in summer but cold, often foggy, weather in winter.

Over the *polar high pressure areas*, air subsides to replace that drawn into the depression circulations, thus completing the large scale up-down-up-down regime in the atmosphere.

This demarcation of pressure zones around the world is complicated by the effects of extreme temperature over large continents. These warm up in summer to create low pressure areas, for instance over central India, but cool drastically in winter to create persistent high pressure areas with dense cold air. Hence the infamous Siberian anticyclone which brings such cold easterly winds to north west Europe and the British Isles.

Food for thought

What is an isobar?

How does the wind blow at 2000 ft in your own hemisphere, according to Buys Ballot's Law?

How does surface wind relate to wind at 2000 ft?

What constant pressure-value chart would you expect to use if flying at 10,000 ft?

In the northern hemisphere, what drift would you expect when flying towards a low pressure centre?

What are convergence and divergence, and why important to weather?

4 Topography and wind behaviour

Pressure gradient winds blow in a generally horizontal manner, but there are many reasons why the simple flow pattern can get confused into turbulent motion. And since air is invisible, it cannot be measured directly, only by its effect upon objects which are visible, and by knowing how it behaves.

A **wind vane** tells the direction of the wind, turning so that its arrow head points to the compass point or angular degree *from which*, it is blowing. Thus a W wind blows from 270° towards an observer, a NW wind blows from 315°. Navigators require the more precise angular definition, but surface wind is usually given by compass point, 16 points giving an adequately realistic measure of accuracy; at ground level wind is never constant because of turbulence. From the air, note surface wind direction from drifting smoke or rippling in corn fields.

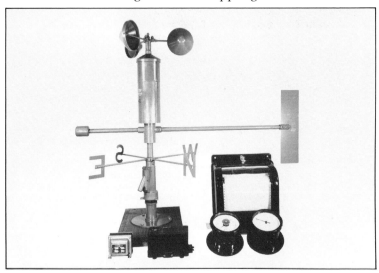

Remote recording anemometer and wind vane, suitable for buildings. The faster the cups rotate, the higher the wind speed. The flat blade of the vane is always blown down-wind, so that the shorter horizontal bar points to the direction **from which** the wind is blowing. *R. W. Munro Ltd.*

BEAUFORT WIND SCALE

Force	Description	Land specifications	Sea specifications	Equivalent speeds Knots	Miles per hour
0	Calm	Smoke rises vertically.	Sea like a mirror.	—	—
1	Light air	Direction of wind shown by smoke drift, but not by wind vanes.	Ripples with the appearance of scales are formed.	1-3	1-3
2	Light breeze	Wind felt on face; leaves rustle, ordinary vane moved by wind.	Small wavelets, still short but more pronounced.	4-6	4-7
3	Gentle breeze	Leaves and small twigs in constant motion; wind extends light flag.	Large wavelets. Crests begin to break.	7-10	8-12
4	Moderate	Raises dust and loose paper, small branches are moved.	Small waves becoming longer, fairly frequent white horses.	11-15	13-18
5	Fresh	Small trees in leaf begin to sway; crest wavelets form on inland waters.	Moderate waves taking a more pronounced long form, many white horses formed. Chance of spray.	16-21	19-24
6	Strong	Large branches in motion; whistling heard in telegraph wires; umbrellas used with difficulty.	Large waves beginning to form; the white foam crests are more extensive everywhere. Probably some spray.	22-27	25-31
7	Near gale	Whole trees in motion; inconvenience felt when walking against wind.	Sea heaps up and white foam from breaking waves begins to be blown in streaks along the direction of the wind.	28-33	32-38
8	Gale	Breaks twigs off trees; generally impedes progress.	Moderately high waves of greater length; edges of crests begin to break into the spindrift.	34-40	39-46
9	Severe gale	Slight structural damage occurs (chimney pots and slates are removed).	High waves. Dense streaks of foam along the direction of the wind. Crests of waves begin to topple, tumble and roll over. Spray may affect visibility.	41-47	47-54
10	Storm	Seldom experienced inland; trees uprooted; considerable structural damage occurs.	Very high waves with long overhanging crests. The resulting foam is blown in dense white streaks along the direction of the wind.	48-55	55-63
11	Violent storm	Widespread damage.	Exceptionally high waves, sometimes concealing small and medium ships. Sea completely covered with long white patches of foam. Edges of wave crests blown into froth. Poor visibility.	56-63	64-73
12	Hurricane	Widespread damage.	Air filled with foam and spray, sea white with driving spray. Visibility bad.	>64	>74

Wind speed cannot be obtained by timing air across a measured distance, though meteorologists approximate to this by tracking balloons blowing freely in the wind. From the air, one can get a good idea of wind speed by watching cloud shadows travelling over the ground on a sunny day, remembering to take account of the height of cloud base above ground.

In 1805 Admiral Sir Francis Beaufort devised a scale of wind strength related to the amount of canvas a sailing vessel could carry in those conditions. This proved to be too dependent upon the subjective decisions of skippers and boats performance, so it was translated into terms of wave heights and sea condition. That worked so well that it was adapted also for landlubbers, wind speed being gauged by the way leaves rustle, trees sway and damage is caused to buildings. The Beaufort scale is still widely used, translated into units of speed, but of course really indicates the power of the wind.

The early pressure plate instruments indicated wind strength by the distance it swung a hinged metal plate over a circular scale; modern cup anemometers indicate wind strength by the number of rotations of the cups around a spindle. A windsock indicates wind direction by turning so that it streams downwind, and blows higher to the horizontal as the wind strength increases — or just hangs limply in calm air!

The force exerted by the wind varies directly as the square of the wind speed. Double the speed in a gust and you quadruple the force exerted upon any object, for instance an aircraft coming in to land. Even motoring across open country can be hazardous in strong gusty winds, specially for high-sided vehicles which present a large cross section towards the wind.

Topography affects wind direction and speed, and since hills and mountains do not blow in the wind, simple knowledge of wind behaviour must replace visible symptoms.

Air cannot stop when it meets high ground, or even a tall block of flats, but must either surmount the obstacle or go around, whichever is the easiest. In this respect it behaves very much like water flowing in a river full of boulders. The fact that high ground obstructs the flow of air means that more of it must crowd into a smaller space to get by, and wind therefore increases in speed to do so. It flows faster over the tops of hills and swirls at above average speed around the ends, often with vicious eddies to leeward. If wind direction is along the line of a valley, it funnels down at increased speed, just like water forced through the restricted nozzle of a hosepipe.

Lift over high ground means motive power for gliders, and this is most effective when the wind direction blows at about 60-90° to the length of the hills or mountains. Lift is smoothest a short

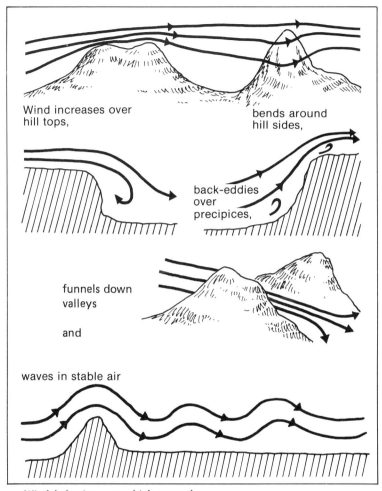

Wind increases over hill tops,

bends around hill sides,

back-eddies over precipices,

funnels down valleys

and

waves in stable air

Wind behaviour near high ground.

distance away from the windward side; there can be turbulent eddies along the top edge of a flat hill, close to the hill slope and near the base. It is well worth spending time watching a river from a bridge, noticing the fluctuations in flow caused by obstructions, and particularly the continuous eddies behind the bridge pillars. It gives you an idea of how to 'see' wind.

Downdraught on the leeward slopes of high ground results from lift on the windward side. What goes up must come down the other side, and since air cannot flow exactly to the contours of a hill side, the 'empty space' close by is filled up with back

There are eddies close to the tops and sides of windward slopes, and dangerous downdraughts on leeward slopes. *M. J. Hammersley*

eddies. Leeward slopes can be very treacherous, even to large powered aircraft, and several unexplained accidents have now been attributed to downdraughts.

Wave motion in air occurs downwind of hill or mountain ranges in certain stable conditions, when warmer air aloft acts as a lid to suppress upward motion. If the wind is fairly strong, 15 kts or more, and blowing across the range, air undulates downwind with a series of crests and troughs which may be shallow or several thousands of feet up into the atmosphere. Lift up to the crests may be negligible or up to 30 ft/sec, according to reported experiences of glider pilots. When the atmosphere is fairly moist, wave crests may be signalled by smooth lens shaped clouds but often there are no such signposts to follow.

Wave motion up into the compressible atmosphere is occasionally mirrored by disastrous downswings towards the non-compressible ground. On 16 February 1962, strong winds undulated across the Pennines and Sheffield had the bad luck to be just below the downswing. A mean wind speed of 65 kts was experienced there in the early hours of the morning, with gusts reaching 84 kts, so that large areas of the town were devastated. A few miles away wind hardly reached 40 kts, sometimes as little as 15 kts.

Flying in waves is often remarkably smooth but there can be extremely turbulent patches near the ground, specially if there are local changes from the general wind direction.

Wind shear is any marked alteration of wind direction or speed over a short distance, either in the vertical or horizontal plane. It can cause marked turbulence within the boundaries of wind change, and is often experienced when coming down to land near deep clouds. Sometimes shear in the upper atmosphere creates clouds which act as signals, but in dry air there need be no visual warning of violent turbulence. Then it is known as Clear Air Turbulence (CAT), which can be particularly unpleasant near the lower boundary of the jet streams.

A shear line de luxe, much relished by glider pilots, occurs in south California, between the Sierra Nevada and the Tehachapi

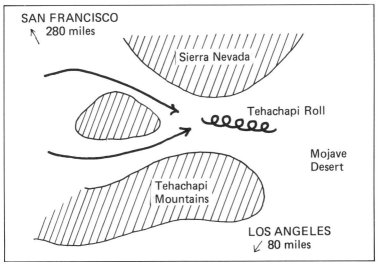

Wind blowing down separate valleys in California produces the Tehachapi Roll. *J. H. Aldrich*

Mts. The pass is about 4000 ft altitude, so that winds approaching from seaward already gain lift in blowing up the mountain sides. In addition, the wind funnels from two directions, W and NW, down separate valleys into the pass. This shear line, or convergence zone creates the Tehachapi Roll, with or without cloud, giving lift on the south side for sometimes 5 miles downwind.

Katabatic winds blow downslope at night when skies are clear and there is little or no pressure wind. Air near hill or mountain side cools, becomes heavier and sinks to create an often appreciable wind. Katabatic winds can begin fairly soon in the evening, and should they blow down opposite slopes of a valley can even create lift over the valley, on the principle that what goes down must force something else up, to make room.

Anabatic winds blow up-slope on calm sunny mornings when the low altitude Sun strikes more effectively at right angles to the hill side than over the plain below. Air warms and rises over the hill, drawing replacement air from the valley and creating an appreciable up-slope wind. This does not always maintain its separate identity once the Sun starts good convection everywhere, but if hills border cool lakes or shaded valley, anabatics can be useful for soaring all day.

The sea breeze develops in coastal areas whenever the Sun is high enough to warm the land appreciably above the temperature of the sea. That means between about April and September in temperate latitudes, but all the year round in the tropics; mostly in bright sunshine but sometimes when the Sun shines weakly through thin cloud.

Warmed air rises over the land, colder air flows in from the sea, while at 2-3000 ft above the land air drifts seawards and sinks, to complete a cellular pattern of air flow in the vertical plane.

As convection continues over the land, the sea breeze gets stronger, blowing directly on-shore at first but tending to veer in the Northern Hemisphere (and back in the Southern) in the afternoon till it blows at about 45° to the coast line. In the British Isles the sea breeze may penetrate 15-20 miles inland and be detectable several miles out at sea, but in hotter climates the wind penetrates much further inland. In complicated areas, like the Solent, where air rises over both the Isle of Wight and the mainland of south England, a sea breeze may operate in both directions to begin with until the stronger wind on to the mainland takes over.

However, the sea breeze often has to come to terms with a larger scale pressure wind. If that, too, is blowing on-shore it

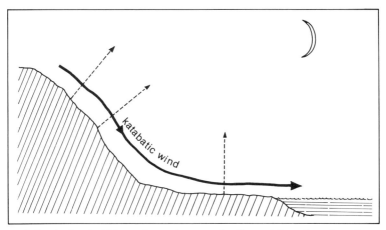

A katabatic wind blows down slope on cloudless nights when there is negligible pressure wind

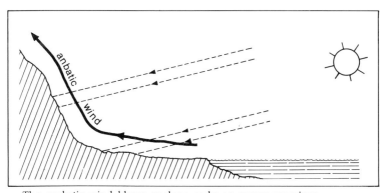

The anabatic wind blows upslope early on sunny mornings

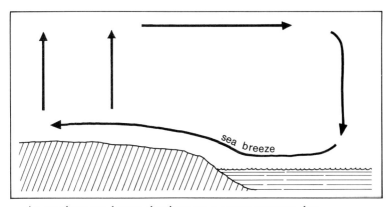

An on-shore sea breeze develops on a sunny summer day

will at first augment the sea breeze but an off-shore pressure wind may counteract an early sea breeze, perhaps for good if the pressure wind is more than 15 kts. Paradoxically, however, later in the day an offshore pressure wind may reinforce the upper seaward air flow and the downdraughts over the sea which feed the sea breeze, and make the latter more effective. Pressure winds which blow at an angle to the shore affect the direction of the sea breeze, but there are no hard and fast rules which apply to all areas. When flying from new airfields near the coast, enquire about the local peculiarities of the sea breeze. Occasionally the sea breeze is marked out by clouds but as often as not it is a matter of searching for lift without any visible signposting.

Food for thought
What is the difference between a W wind and one from 270°?
How does the force of the wind vary with its speed?
What surface wind speed would you expect on hearing a gale warning?
What is the wind hazard over lee slopes?
What is wind shear?
What is a katabatic wind?
Over what kind of terrain could anabatics be useful for soaring?
In what months of the year can one hope for sea breezes in temperate latitudes?
How does the sea breeze change in direction during the day?

Contrail persisting to form cloud.

Hoar frost on leaves. *M. J. Hammersley.*

5 Water in the atmosphere

All the wet manifestations of weather are produced from one basic supply of water in the world which gets re-cycled over and over again. Water evaporates from seas, rivers and lakes (using up heat to do so); vapour condenses again as dew, fog or cloud (and releases some heat in the process). Rain falls from clouds, percolating through the soil back to the sea, or is absorbed by plants and transpired again as vapour from foliage. Quite apart from condensation and evaporation tricks, water transforms itself into solid state when temperatures are low. The problem for aviators is that many flights cover large distances, through flight levels having variable temperatures, so that every disguise of water may be encountered in one day.

Water vapour is always present in air, even on a fine day. It is acquired mainly from the oceans, and if air has had a long journey across the sea it will be much more moist than if the wind has travelled across a continent.

Water vapour resides in the atmosphere in variable quantities, rather like guests in a hotel. The warmer the air (or larger the hotel) the more vapour (or guests) can be accommodated, but only up to a certain maximum capacity, fixed for every temperature (or each hotel).

It is the circumstances of past history which dictate whether air (or hotel) is full up with vapour or undercapacity.

Relative Humidity (RH) is the amount of water vapour actually present in air expressed as a percentage of the maximum possible at that air temperature. Air is saturated when RH is 100%, and then can absorb no more vapour until air temperature rises again.

RH can change either because of alteration in air temperature or because of changes in vapour content, or both. An aircraft engine emits both water vapour and heat from the exhaust. If the vapour emission is not offset by the heat effect, a condensation trail (*contrail*) forms behind each engine, and may be persistent if the atmosphere is already moist. Occasionally when the heat released outweighs the moisture factor, an aircraft flying through cloud dissipates some of the droplets, to create a clear passage or hole in the cloud called a (*distrail*).

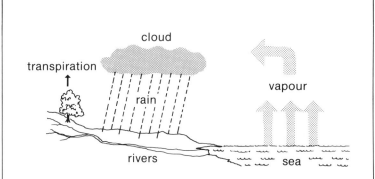

The water cycle processes one global supply over and over again, by evaporation from the seas, condensation as cloud and precipitation, transpiration of vapour from plants, and return of water in rivers to the seas again.

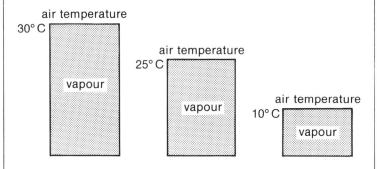

Warm air *can* hold more vapour than cold air.

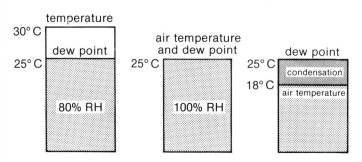

When clear air, less than saturated cools to dew point, further cooling causes condensation.

Dew-point is the temperature at which air becomes saturated, given its particular vapour content. When RH is 100%, dew point is the same as air temperature and any further cooling results in vapour being deposited as condensation. Parked aircraft collect dew quickly because metal cools rapidly on still cloudless nights; grass collects dew quickly because the air close to it always has a high RH because of transpiration of vapour from the blades.

Hoar frost is deposited directly out of air when the temperature falls below a dewpoint which is less than 0°C. It affects aircraft which have been flying at sub-zero temperatures and then descend into clear air which has a dew point as cold or colder than the plane. Hoar frost on the windscreen suddenly cuts visibility, and this only clears once the temperature of the aircraft has risen to that of the warmer air.

Water starts to freeze at a temperature of 0°C, or lower if it is salty. The process of freezing releases a certain amount of latent heat which delays the solidification of water and makes it a gradual affair. Water drops, however, when individually held in suspension in fog or cloud, can remain liquid at temperatures much lower, even as far as -30°C, and are then said to be supercooled.

Supercooled water drops have a precarious existence because contact with subfreezing particles, surfaces or aircraft causes them to solidify. They freeze immediately into crystals if the droplets are very small but only gradually if the drops are large, when part of each drop crystallises and the remainder freezes more slowly.

Rime is the crust of ice crystals which builds up on trees, gates and fences when small supercooled water droplets in fog colder than 0°C drift past these obstructions. It builds up on the windward sides, each ice crystal freezing the next supercooled water droplet which settles upon it. Likewise, an aircraft flying through cloud having small supercooled droplets will induce rime to build up along all the leading surfaces. Rime is often loosely packed so that much may brush off in the airflow.

Cloudy ice forms on aircraft flying through cloud having larger supercooled water drops. Part of each drop freezes at once into rime crystals, the temperature of the remainder is raised by the latent heat released and runs back over the wings to freeze more slowly into clear ice. The cloudy mixture can build up very quickly into a dangerous weight affecting the performance of an aircraft.

Glazed frost is more dangerous still. There are occasions, to be discussed later, when rain falls from cloud into a layer of air having subzero temperature, freezing on impact with all

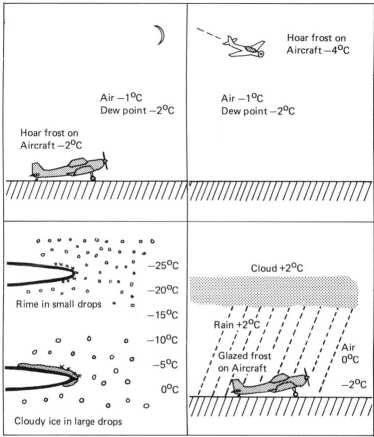

Air −1°C
Dew point −2°C

Hoar frost on
Aircraft −2°C

Hoar frost on
Aircraft −4°C

Air −1°C
Dew point −2°C

−25°C
−20°C
Rime in small drops
−15°C
−10°C
−5°C
0°C
Cloudy ice in large drops

Cloud +2°C

Rain +2°C

Glazed frost
on Aircraft

Air
0°C

−2°C

Types of icing liable to be encountered when flying at temperatures below 0°C.

subzero surfaces. Weight of ice builds up quickly, and such a zone is no place to be flying.

Evaporation is the process by which water or water drops are returned to air as invisible vapour. Even ice crystals can be vaporised without going through the melt stage, a process called sublimation.

Both evaporation and sublimation require heat, either extracted from the air itself or from the surface on which the water is lying. Hence the thermostatic control system of the human body, which maintains normal temperature in hot weather by the evaporation of sweat.

A wet-and-dry bulb thermometer uses the principle of cooling by evaporation in order to evaluate the dew point of air. The instrument consists of two identical thermometers mounted

Tabular iceberg in Marguerite Bay, Antarctica, with a helicopter from HMS *Endurance*, February 1973. There is very little annual precipitation in polar regions because the air is too cold to hold much vapour. But whatever does fall, a few inches per year, lies refrigerated for centuries, showing up as compacted striations in the ice. *Courtesy HMS Endurance, Crown Copyright*

Thick rime and cloudy ice accumulated on the windward side of a gate after supercooled cloud had covered the hill in a strong wind.
M. J. Hammersley

side by side, one of which has its bulb covered in muslin which is kept wet by a wick dipped into distilled water. Evaporation of the water from the muslin extracts heat from the wet bulb, whose reading is therefore always lower than that of the dry bulb thermometer. The drier the air the greater the evaporation rate from the muslin and the greater the difference between the two readings. When the air is saturated both thermometers read the same.

Relative humidity and dew point can be evaluated from tables supplied with such an instrument. Dew point is approximately as far below the wet bulb temperature as the latter is below the dry bulb temperature.

Food for thought
What is the basic ingredient of all the visible water products of weather?
What is relative humidity?
What happens if air temperature cools to dew point?
What are supercooled water drops, and in what temperature range can they exist in cloud?
What is rime and how does it differ from cloudy ice?
What happens to the temperature of the immediate environment when water evaporates?

6 Fog, by contact with cold surfaces.

Fog forms when air cools over a surface which is colder than the dew point of the air. There are two ways in which this can happen, and fog is named accordingly, even though the end products are the same.

Advection fog forms when air travels from a warmer region and reaches a surface already colder than dew point. For instance, a change in wind direction bringing a thaw after a cold winter spell nearly always results in fog forming over frosted land or snow. The air cools to dew point, condensation occurs throughout a fairly thick layer of air, and fog only disperses when the new warmer air raises the temperature of the ground itself.

Sea fog is a type of advection fog, forming within an airstream which travels from a warmer latitude into a region where the sea is colder than the dew-point of air. It is a frequent occurrence in the south west approaches to the UK in early spring, when the sea is at its coldest, but sea fog can form at any

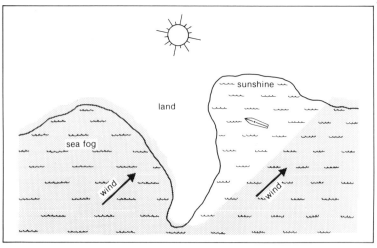

Sea fog may clear after a short passage across warming land in summer

time of the year. In high summer, even in a heat wave, warm air blowing off the land and having a long sea track, perhaps down the North Sea or along the English Channel, may induce fog.

Advection fogs can persist in quite fresh wind, because turbulence merely brings more air of the same dew point down to the surface, where it cools. It requires a radical change in wind direction to clear these fogs. However, if sea fog drifts across the land in summer it quickly clears over the warmer land. Holiday-makers may find sunshine a very short distance inland, even to leeward of a headland.

From the air, sea fog delineates the coast line fairly precisely in summer and this distinguishes it from other types of cloud when seen from above. In winter, the land may be as cold or colder than the sea, in which case sea fog drifts inland and persists there too. If wind is more than 10 kts, sea fog may be lifted off the surface of sea or land to form a low ceiling of shapeless cloud called stratus. That makes all the difference to sea traffic or motor traffic, but gives little room to manoeuvre for landing aircraft. Stratus and fog look alike from the air. **Radiation mist and fog** forms when fairly stagnant air cools to dew point over a surface which is itself cooling. This means the land, cooling by radiation heat loss under clear skies at night. The wind must be not so strong as to prevent air lying in contact with the ground for a while, but light enough to stir the air and spread cooling throughout a layer above the ground. About 2-3 kts; a dead calm probably produces dew on the ground only.

Radiation fog is most likely in winter, when there are long

Mist clinging low to field after a still clear night. Tree tops are above the inversion level, in air warmer than the air near the ground.

nights; most likely when the ground is wet after rain or close to humid areas like lakes and rivers. It forms patchily, because land temperatures are rarely exactly the same, and gradually thickens into a continuous blanket. Patchiness is a particular problem when motoring. One can drive out of a clear town on to damp heathland where fog is starting to form and where a starry night with superb visibility alternates abruptly with blinding fog patches.

Fog forms soonest in low lying hollows and valleys, because it is a product of cooling air, which flows down hill. Tops of buildings may stand clear of fog, so may factory chimneys, and so may airfields on high ground where landing conditions may be perfect despite the obliteration of lower ground by fog.

Clearance of radiation fog may be achieved by the sudden change in wind direction bringing drier air, or even by strengthening of wind speed. However, in summer the principal clearance agent is the Sun which burns off the fog and reverses the inversion of temperature beneath which the fog formed the night before. This probably happens so early in the morning that one hardly realises fog has occured. In spring and autumn, however, where days and nights are of more equal length, fog may persist till mid-morning before the power of the Sun can shift it. It often re-forms again the next night, and in settled periods may clear and form again to an almost routine timetable.

In winter, the Sun may be unequal to the task of clearing fog at all, in which case it may persist for days on end until there is a radical change in wind direction and pressure pattern.

High level airfields are in a tricky situation when radiation fog starts to clear. They may have stood clear of fog in the valleys all night, but when the Sun rises it quickly warms the exposed hill side and produces an upslope anabatic wind. This helps stir up the fog below which can quite suddenly pour over the airfield

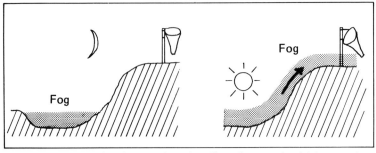

On calm clear nights fog may form in valleys, but envelop high ground next morning.

blanketing everything temporarily. This particular danger gives special meaning to the saying 'it came right out of the blue'. Fog is about the only weather which can sneak up without any other warning than is given by theoretical knowledge.

Supercooled fog consists of liquid water drops having a temperature of 0°C or less. Before thinking about how to fly, worry about how to get to the airfield. The roads will be ice rinks, car windscreens will be opaque with ice and you probably can't even get the key into the door lock!

Food for thought

How does advection fog form and what causes it to clear?
In what wind and cloud conditions can you expect radiation fog?
In what areas would you expect radiation fog to form first?
What is the danger to high level airfields of having fog in the valleys below?
How would you react to a forecast of supercooled fog?

7 Clouds by lift over high ground

Clouds, and the water products which fall from them, are created by a cooling mechanism more powerful than mere contact with a cold surface; *adiabatic cooling* of air. 'Adiabatic' comes from the Greek language, meaning *shall not pass through* and an adiabatic change of temperature is one achieved without any give or take of heat. This sounds less like Double Dutch if one considers two familiar domestic examples.

The temperature of a gas, like air, rises when it is compressed. Hence, when pumping a bicycle tyre, even on a cold or cloudy day, the compressed air inside the pump becomes hotter and also makes the pump warm to touch. Conversely, when a gas expands because of a reduction in pressure, its temperature falls. For instance, gas released from compression out of a gas cartridge into a soda syphon makes the cartridge temporarily too cold to handle comfortably, even though a moment before it was at room temperature.

Carburettor icing is a consequence of the same sort of gas behaviour. Expansion of air through the carburettor, together with evaporation of fuel, can lead to a temperature drop in the fuel and air mixture of about 20 Celsius degrees. Water vapour in the air condenses and freezes to ice on the inside of the carburettor. On dry days, or when the air temperature is below

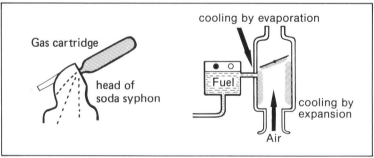

All gases cool on expansion, eg, when released from a gas cartridge into a soda siphon or air expanding when forced into the chamber of a carburettor.

about -10°C, vapour is deposited directly as frost crystals which may pass through the engine without adhering to the inside. It must be emphasised that carburettor icing can occur in clear air, a function of invisible vapour and air temperature, so it is no good looking for visual warning, such as cloud or rain, though of course carburettor icing can occur in cloud too.

Atmospheric pressure is the compression and expansion agent in the weather context. When air is forced to rise upwards it experiences reduced atmospheric pressure, expands and cools. If air temperature falls to a dew point, some vapour condenses out to form a cloud base. When air sinks, on the other hand, atmospheric pressure upon it increases so that temperature rises, sometimes becoming warmer than dew point when cloud droplets start to evaporate.

Stratus forms when air is very moist, so that it cools to dew point before reaching the summit, low on the windward slope. The cloud covers the hill so that anyone walking there experiences fog, and the cloud is often called hill fog.

A cap cloud forms over the summit on drier days when air fails to reach dew-point at a lower level. The cloud appears oddly stationary when a fresh wind is blowing, because it does not travel with the wind. It continually forms to windward and disperses in the sinking air to leeward, with the wind blowing through the constantly changing conglomeration of cloud drops.

Lenticular clouds often form in the crests of wave motion downwind of hill and mountain ranges, marking out the undulating wind for those looking for lift. Often the humidity in upper layers of air varies, so that one can see a 'pile of plates', lens clouds formed in moist layers with clear air between.

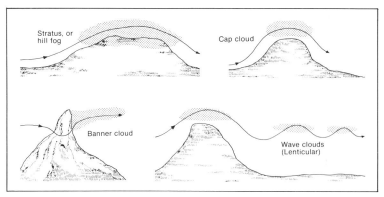

Orographic clouds, formed by expansion, cooling and condensation from air forced to lift over high ground

Rotor clouds sometimes form in the turbulent eddies on the leeward side of mountains, and can be exceedingly turbulent. *Banner clouds* stream from mountain peaks, when air finds it easier to blow around the obstruction rather than over the top. Air is lifted upwards in back eddies and when the air is moist at

Orographic cloud, formed by lift over mountain, with air cooling to dew point just above the summit.

that level, forms a banner blowing downwind and dispersing gradually with distance from the peaks. The Matterhorn, Mt Teide, Mt Fujima and all other famous world peaks display banner clouds sometimes when skies are otherwise cloudless. Remember, however, that the turbulent eddies will also exist even when the whole sky is masked by cloud.

Local names for orographic clouds abound, and it is always sensible when flying in a new area to talk to local inhabitants about their peculiarities of cloud and weather. Stratus is 'Scotch mist' in Scotland, 'mizzle' in Devon, 'the Table Cloth' over Table Mountain outside Cape Town. The Crossfell range in the north of England carries a 'Helm' over the summit in a strong northeasterly wind, while a 'Helm Bar' appears in the turbulent rotary eddy downwind.

Drizzle or light rain sometimes falls from orographic cloud, mainly on the windward slope and over the top. In that case, air descending on the far side and warming by compression at the saturated lapse rate reaches dew point sooner than it was reached on cooling on the windward slope. Cloud base will be higher and the new clear air will have longer to warm adiabatically at the higher, dry lapse rate. By the time air reaches ground level, the temperature will be higher than it was when it began ascent the other side.

A Fohn wind is a warm dry wind down steep slopes on occasions when there is a temperature inversion over the heights. A Fohn may blow even when there is no loss of moisture, as described in the last paragraph, and is often warmer than can be explained by compression of the original air alone. It seems that the strong wind over the mountain top sucks down air from above the inversion, already warm, which is warmed still further by compression on descent with the original air. The name Fohn was given originally to the wind experienced in the European Alps, but is now applied generically to all similar winds.

Food for thought

What happens when a gas expands due to reduction in pressure?

Why does carburettor icing occur, and in what weather?

How does stratus form?

How does the base height of stratus differ on the leeward slope from that on the windward slope?

What do lenticular clouds downwind of a mountain range indicate?

8 Lift in thermals giving cumulus clouds

Thermals can be the most powerful source of lift in the whole weather scene, depending upon the heat source and the temperature gradient of the atmosphere on any particular day.

There are two stages to creation of a thermal

1. *Air warms* by conduction of heat when lying close to a surface which is itself warming. The thin layer of air expands, its density falls and eventually a bubble of air breaks away from the surface and starts to rise. Moving traffic, obstacles on the ground or even the wind helps the bubble to break free from the super-heated layer. It is replaced near the ground by colder heavier air from alongside or from above, which then takes its turn to warm by contact with the surface.

   The Sun is the primary heat source, mainly in summer in the temperate latitudes, but there are subsidiary sources like erupting volcanoes, forest fires, burning stubble, power stations, even warm dirt particles in a thick haze layer.

   Surfaces which heat best but also cool rapidly again when the Sun sets, are dry sand, rock, soil, concrete, tarmac and tiled roofs, specially when sloping towards the Sun. Wet surfaces do not warm so quickly, neither does vegetation which is mainly water.

   The sea hardly changes temperature at all in any day, but nevertheless can be a thermal trigger, when cold air travels across it into latitudes where the sea is already warmer.

2. *Air cools* once it has started to rise into the atmosphere, for no other reason than that the atmospheric pressure upon it is reduced. Provided that the bubble of air remains warmer than its surroundings, despite being itself subjected to cooling, it will be buoyant in the atmosphere and continue to rise. Once it becomes colder than its surroundings the air bubble ceases to rise. Some bubbles don't get far and quickly mix with the surrounding air; others combine to form a column of rising air, invisible but well documented in recent years by reports from glider pilots who have flown in them.

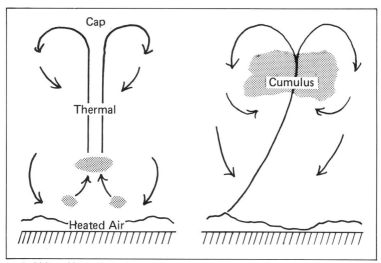

| Bubbles of heated air close to the ground rise, join with others and create a rising thermal of air. | When rising air cools to dew point, cloud forms and builds up so long as rising air remains buoyant in its surroundings. |

Thermal bubbles flatten at the top and stretch sideways as they rise and mix at the edges with the environment air, to become something the shape of mushrooms with stalks. There is a central core of strongest upcurrent and at the cap, the limit of the thermal, air flows outwards and down again. There is some evidence of spiralling movement too, either clockwise or anticlockwise.

Cumulus with crisp tops developing over the distant shore. The land is a thermal source, but not the sea.

Fair weather cumulus, at maximum development around midday. Dry thermals to about 5000 ft, shallow clouds only with plenty of blue sky between for the parachutist to see where he wants to drop. *Alan James*

Thermals may be disrupted by strong winds, but often maintain a distorted but still effective core, leaning in the wind as that changes with height. Rising currents in clear air are called dry thermals, but the deeper more active thermals are nearly always signposted by cumulus clouds.

Cumulus clouds form as soon as rising air cools below dew point, when a cloud base forms. When the lower atmosphere is well mixed and fairly dry all cloud bases may be as high as 4-6000 ft above ground, and look as level as if cut off with a knife.

Cloud continues to build upwards so long as the thermal is buoyant in the atmosphere. Cloud top marks the limit, or cap, of the thermal after which the cumulus disperses in downcurrents and another cloud develops in an adjacent thermal. Small cumulus may last only a few minutes, but the largest, called cumulonimbus which give showers, may have a life of about 40 minutes. Sometimes cumulus become organised into evenly spaced lines, called 'Streets'.

Over land, cumulus follow the fortunes of the Sun, starting life when the Sun rises, attain peak development by early afternoon and disperse again when the Sun sets. If the Sun gets hidden by sheet cloud, so that thermals cease before their usual evening time, then cumulus too disperse.

Over the sea, whose temperature does not change appreciably in 24 hours, cumulus do not disperse at night. If the sea is warm enough to trigger themals by day it does the same at night. However, when the wind blows on-shore, cumulus may drift across the coast long after those inland have dispersed to leave a clear night.

Although cumulus clouds are only composed of water drops, they can sometimes act as obstacles to the wind, which may undulate across them.

Vertical winds can be detected by the contours of cumulus clouds. Well defined bases with crisp bubbling tops show that thermals are still pushing upwards; if the tops become blurred they are evaporating into warming air and thermals, still active into cloud base, are becoming shallower.

When cumulus have both blurred bases and tops, then thermals are collapsing, either because the Sun is setting or because it is being obscured by higher cloud.

Large cumulus, typical of vigorous thermals in unstable airstream.

The taller a cumulus and larger the base area, the stronger the vertical wind speed. Weak thermals are about 1.5-3 ft/sec, but fairly large clouds may contain lift of about 9 ft/sec. Daring research flights into cumulonimbus have shown updraughts of 50 ft/sec, occasionally 85 ft/sec.

What goes up must come down, in the clear spaces between clouds and along the outer edge of cumulus where water drops evaporate into the environment. Some of the descending air gets sucked again into the bottom of clouds, condenses and release latent heat to give a few minutes more life to the cloud. The combination of ascending air in the centre of the cumulus and descent with evaporation on the outer edges often gives a concave shape to the cloud base, clear air with a fringe of fuzzy cloud around.

What goes up in a cumulonimbus large enough to give a shower may also come down within cloud with very nasty force, and will be dealt with in the next chapter.

The depth of thermals and cumulus clouds can be forecast from the temperature profile of the day, ie, the rate at which temperature of the atmosphere decreases with height, as determined by radio sonde upper air ascents. Every day the graph of temperature-with-altitude is unique. Warm air, which has cooled near the ground en route to colder latitudes, has a steeper profile than cold air, which has benefitted near the ground by travel over with warmer surfaces. These temperature profiles of the environment are never smooth curves. On average temperature decreases with height at about 2 Celsius degrees per 1000 ft, but sometimes the rates are more, sometimes less, a matter of circumstance and past history.

Rising air in a thermal, however, is a very short term event and cools more like a laboratory experiement, at known rates. Air cools at just over 3 Celsius degrees per 1000 ft when unsaturated, rather less within cloud when saturated, because the process of condensation releases latent heat to counteract the temperature decrease. Forecasters can determine temperature change in a thermal, given ground temperature, humidity and MSL pressure, from a series of graphs depicting these dry and saturated adiabatic lapse rates.

It is the intersection of the lapse rate curve of the thermal with the temperature profile of the day which determines the depth of cumulus clouds, because that point indicates where thermal air becomes colder than its surroundings.

Look at the two profiles illustrated, for two separate days but each by chance having the same air temperature near the ground. On both occasions air cools first at the straight line, dry lapse rate, and then as a smooth curve when saturated; but the

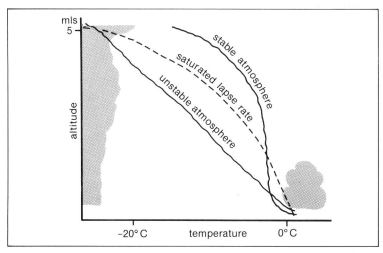

Cumulus develop up to the level at which rising air in a thermal becomes colder than its surroundings. This occurs sooner in stable air than in unstable air.

cloud top occurs much sooner in the stable atmosphere (steep graph) than in the unstable atmosphere (flatter graph), where cloud soars several miles high.

There are some occasions when developing cumulus spread out under a stable layer of air to become a continuous sheet of

Stratocumulus formed from cumulus spreading out beneath an inversion.

A lenticular cloud, in a stable and drier layer of air above cumulus clouds.

stratocumulus. That disrupts thermal activity by cutting out the Sun, until the cloud sheet later breaks into pancake shapes and disperses because of small scale convection processes within the cloud. Then thermal activity can start all over again, and under a higher altitude Sun.

Pressure patterns and latitudinal differences govern the occurrence of cumulus clouds. There are very few cumulus, and only shallow, in the high pressure belt which encircles the world in the sub-tropics.

In temperate latitudes, the most unstable atmospheres are deep polar airstreams blowing towards warmer latitudes behind depressions. Stable atmospheres, without any frontal cloud disrupting thermal activity, occur in ridges of high pressure between depressions and in fully established anticyclones. Cumulus clouds are then shallow or non-existent, and the only thermals are dry ones.

In Equatorial regions, where the tropopause is very high and where the warm air contains abundant vapour from which to produce condensation with release of latent heat, cumulus clouds soar as high as 60,000 ft.

In Polar latitudes, cumulus are rare and mainly over the dry valleys. When they develop, tops are usually no more than 6000 ft; apart from the fact that the Sun has so little power as a thermal trigger, the air is too cold to hold much vapour for condensation.

Food for thought
How does a thermal begin life?
What kind of surfaces produce the best thermals?
What is a dry thermal?

When does rising air in a thermal produce cloud?
What are two reasons for the dispersal of cumulus clouds?
When do cumulus form over the sea?
What is the temperature profile of the atmosphere?
Which has the greatest lapse rate, a dry thermal or one in cloud?
Which temperature profile has the steeper slope, stable or unstable air?
Which wind direction presages the biggest cumulus in the UK?

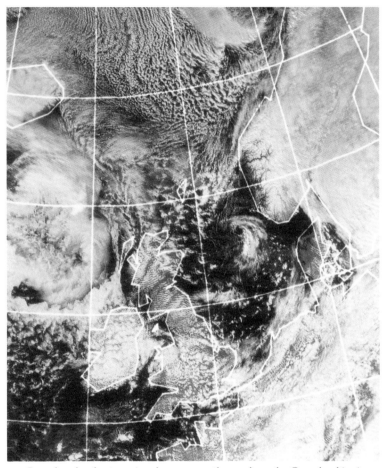

Cumulus clouds streaming down across the sea from the Greenland ice in northerly winds. Close streets of cumulus, together with a street of vortices downwind from Jan Mayen Island. Over Scotland and northern England clouds arranged in wave patterns by lift over high ground. Large cumulus developing over the Midland and central Ireland. Satellite picture, on visible wavelength, taken from NOAA 9 at 1336 GMT on 27.3.85. *Courtesy of Dundee University*

9 Cumulonimbus and showers

There is as much difference between fair weather cumulus and cumulonimbus as there is between an infant and a wrestler. Same breed, same origin, but having no similarity as regards strength, although one may grow into the other when conditions are ripe.

Cumulonimbus, which are colloquially called cunimb, grow from small fleeces to huge cauliflower shapes, whose crisp billowing outlines continually change and pinpoint the soaring air currents. Spend some time just looking at these giants, because the changing contours tell a vivid tale of power.

Cauliflower clouds may grow further to become huge towers, with very white dense-looking tops composed of ice crystals, often drawn out by stronger upper winds into anvil shapes. Cloud tops may be anything from 15,000 ft to 30,000 ft and near the Equator perhaps nearer 60,000 ft. Cloud base is generally much lower than in fair weather cumulus, about 1500 ft above

Cumulonimbus seen in full depth, blowing along the coast from left to right of the picture. Anvil tops indicate the clouds which are on the wane; adjacent billowing cells still soaring upwards.

ground with patchy cloud below 1000 ft in the turbulent moist air into which a shower may be falling.

On very active convection days one cannot always see these cunimb in full vertical extent because the whole sky is a chaotic assembly of cloud bases, one cunimb following another in quick succession. Cloud colours then range from almost black directly underneath, through every shade of grey, with the merest glimpse of bright white high-level cloud between the packed clouds.

Precipitation from clouds is not a simple matter of continued condensation until water drops get large enough to fall to ground. For one thing, there is a limit to the size of any individual water drop, about 2.5 mm radius, beyond which the drop breaks up into several. Moreover, if droplets can remain in suspension in fog and cloud, without coalescing to fall to ground, there must be some other reason for their descent, specially when cunimb clouds have such strong upcurrents as support.

Ice provides part of the answer. Clouds consist of supercooled water drops, with a few ice crystals present at air temperatures around $-10°C$, more at temperatures of $-20°C$. At about $-30°C$ ice crystals usually constitute the whole cloud layer, and this final *glaciation* takes place very quickly. Supercooled water drops freeze first on the outside, and then burst when the inside also freezes and expands, thus providing many more ice nucleii on which the remaining supercooled drops can crystallise.

Ice crystals latch together to form snowflakes of greater weight than individual water drops and eventually become large enough to fall against the lift in cloud. When the $0°C$ isotherm is close to ground they fall as snow, but if the $0°C$ isotherm is high the snow melts to become rain.

There is some coalescence of water drops and snowflakes to assist in the production of rain, because flakes and drops have different sizes and reach different terminal speeds in fall. Those which travel faster scoop up smaller drops on the way till they attain their possible maximum size.

As a general rule, the change in appearance of the upper part of a large cumulus, to become a more fibrous white, indicates glaciation and a sign that a shower is imminent.

Hail forms when snowflakes or water drops cannot beat the upcurrents within a cunimb at first attempt but are tossed up and down, alternately melting and refreezing to become balls of ice which are heavy enough to fall. Single stones usually consist of concentric layers of clear and cloudy ice, looking rather like the growth rings which develop in a tree trunk. In the UK hail is

Assorted hail from a storm at Christchurch, New Zealand.
M. J. Hammersley

most frequent in summer, when cunimb are largest, and stones
are usually about pea size, occasionally as big as golf balls. In
Equatorial regions, specially in mountainous area where there
is extra lift to accentuate thermals, hailstones can attain
grapefruit size. Hailstones can coalesce within cloud to form
lethal lumps of ice, but any hail can be devastating ammunition
when pounding an aircraft.

Icing within a cunimb is usually more severe than in other
types of cloud, because larger water drops get carried upwards
into colder zones which usually only have small drops which
freeze to rime. Cloudy ice can quickly coat any aircraft, or even
any pilot unfortunate enough to have to parachute down within
a cunimb. In 1930 five glider pilots had to bale out of their craft
over the Rhon mountains in Germany, and were carried up and
down within supercooled cunimb, until they were encapsu-
lated in ice on reaching ground. Only one man survived the
ordeal.

Thunder and lightning often accompany the other violence of a
cunimb. Glaciation in the cloud triggers separation of electrical
charge, the positive collecting at the top of the cloud and
negative near the base, often near the −10°C isotherm.

Eventually there is discharge as lightning, together with thunder which is the sound of the violent expansion of air heated along the line of flash. There is much research still to be done before meteorologists fully understand the electrification of clouds.

Winds near a cunimb are exceedingly confused because of the contrary horizontal and vertical winds involved.

a) The cloud itself travels on the pressure wind of the day, usually steered by the wind blowing at about 10,000 ft. It continues inexorably in that direction, whatever contrary impressions are given by wind shear near the ground.

b) Upcurrents into the leading edge of the cunimb suck in air from near the ground, so that the surface wind which has previously prevailed is suddenly reversed. This shear results in a very turbulent gust line, often marked by a roll cloud.

c) Precipitation falling through cloud cools the air and creates a strong cold downdraught which smacks to ground like water from a tap, spreading outwards in all directions. Then cloud base often droops with udder shaped contours, called mammata, as the downdraughts carry cloud temporarily with them. These protruberances evaporate as soon as they are warmed by compression on descent and mix with the environment air.

d) Finally, behind the cunimb, wind settles back into a normal pattern again, but that is always gusty on a day of strong convection. The up-and-down motion in the atmosphere means that air is continually being brought down to ground from

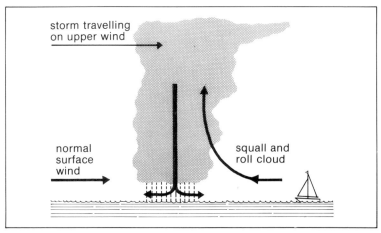

Surface wind is sucked towards the leading edge of an approaching storm, becomes particularly violent and changeable near the squall line, and may change yet again in the downblast of cold air and precipitaion from the centre of the cloud.

Radiation fog in valleys, early morning. *M. J. Hammersley*

A glory, seen on sea fog in Lyttelton Harbour, New Zealand, by an observer standing on a hill above, with the sun setting behind him. Colours similar to those of a corona. Glories are often seen around the shadow of an aircraft flying just above cloud consisting of small regular sized water drops. *M. J. Hammersley*

Stratus cloud (lifted fog) breaking into diffuse patches and about to disperse altogether

Cloud streak, stretched from one quarter of the sky to the other, persisting from an aircraft contrail about an hour earlier. Cirrus was drawn out by wind and melted to form cellular altocumulus.

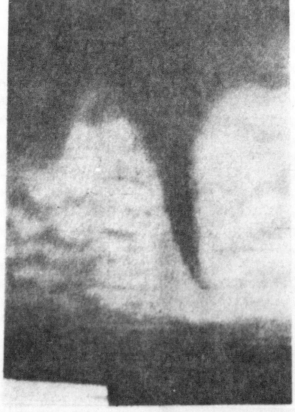

Funnel cloud descending from a storm cloud over Berkshire on 21 May 1950. The worst damage caused by the tornado was at Linslade, near Leighton Buzzard, where two rows of houses were almost entirely unroofed. *Leighton Buzzard Observer*

higher levels, where speed is usually stronger and direction different.

All these various elements to the wind pattern near a cunimb result in extremely difficult conditions for takeoff or landing. The extreme wind shears may give a head wind one moment and a tail wind the next; prepare for anything but keep clear if possible till the shower passes, which it often does quite quickly.

The amount of rain or snow falling from a cunimb can be very great but is usually concentrated in a short period of 10-15 minutes. It can create aquaplaning conditions on roads and runways, severely taxes the capacity of gutters and drains, and often runs off soil surfaces before having time to penetrate. The 'gentle rain from heaven', which persists for several hours and benefits crops and gardens, falls from a different kind of cloud called altostratus.

Tornadoes sometimes form within very large cunimb, intense vortices of spiralling air which must serve in some way to augment these powerhouses of energy. The vortices lower from the main cloud base as funnel clouds, having very low pressure at the centre and extremely strong winds around the core. These clouds do not always lower to ground, but when they do they suck up all manner of debris and cause buildings to explode because of the difference in external and internal pressure. Tornadoes are to be avoided at all costs, and not to be confused with similar looking vortices, *dust devils* which form under clear skies and over very hot surfaces. Over the hot plains of North America dust devils can rise several hundred feet, made visible by lifted dust and sand, and experienced glider pilots can fly them. *Water spouts* are tornadoes descending from cunimb over the sea.

Food for thought
How does an anvil top differ from cloud near the base of a cunimb?
What is glaciation and what does it herald in a cunimb?
How does hail form?
What wind shears are present beneath a cunimb?
How do tornadoes, water spouts and dust devils differ from each other?

A banner cloud streaming from the Matterhorn, Switzerland. *F. Ross*

Temporary cloud formed in an anabatic (upslope) wind in early morning on the Isle of Capri.

A 'pile of plates,' wave clouds over the Rock and Pillar Range, Otago, New Zealand. *M. J. Hammersley*

10 Cloud and rain in convergent winds around low pressure.

Convergent winds which meet along a well defined boundary form a *front*, that word being used in the battle sense. The different airs cannot mix together at once, so the heavier undercuts less dense and warmer air, which is lifted upwards. Expansion and cooling to dew point follows.

A sea breeze front exists when the cold wind from the sea conflicts with an opposite warmer pressure wind over the land. In very dry conditions there may be no marker clouds to

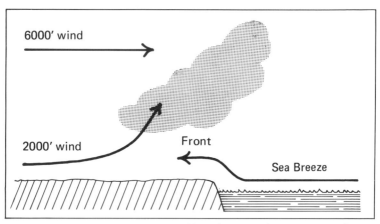

A sea breeze front forms when a cold sea breeze undercuts an opposing warm wind from inland, forming a line of cumulus.

indicate the wind shear and lift, but on many occasions a line of cumulus forms along the front. Very occasionally the frontal clouds will give a shower. When the pressure wind is very light the sea breeze can carry the front well inland, but if the wind at around 2000 ft is appreciable, the cumulus clouds may be blown to the seaward side of the front, and the lift be along a sloping plane.

An intertropical front exists when converging winds either side of the Equator meet, providing some lift and convection clouds.

However, the temperature contrast between winds in the intertropical convergence zone is not usually great, and the front much less well defined than when contrasting airs meet in middle latitudes.

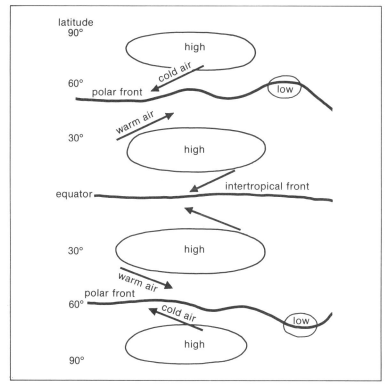

Major fronts around the world

A Polar front is the battle line between cold winds from Polar regions and much warmer subtropical winds. The initial front waves in fluid fashion, and atmospheric pressure falls at the tip. The wave sometimes runs harmlessly along the front, but more often grows to exaggerated size with a complete wind circulation around the low pressure centre. This is a *depression* of the temperate latitudes, one of many vortex solutions of the natural world, like spinning water down a bath plug hole! The battle between the air masses results in a recognisable sequence of clouds and rain, as a sector of warm air is undercut by pursuing deep cold air and is forced to slither upwards over cool air ahead.

A large cumulus top protruding through a lower layer of stratified cloud. All cumulus have unique contours, and never again is one likely to see such a 'cumulus coiffure'. *G. Uveges*

Cumulonimbus, with dense cirrus top, giving shower. *M. J. Hammersley*

A street of shallow cumulus, typical of high pressure weather, blowing downwind from some thermal source.

Squall line at the leading edge of a cumulonimbus. *M. J. Hammersley*

A cold front is the surface boundary between cold air and warm air ahead which it is undercutting. The cold air thrusts beneath the warm with such vigour that it triggers a line of cunimb, with their usual violent showers, perhaps hail and thunder too. The cold front usually moves quickly and passes any one area in well under an hour, but it may arrive at any time of day or night, being independent of thermal activity.

A cold front moves at the speed of the pressure gradient wind behind it, providing that is at right-angles to the front. When the following wind blows at an angle to the front, then only the component at right-angles to the front is useful in pushing it along. The front nearly always travels faster near the centre of a depression than on the periphery, where it trails behind.

Cold front approaching, with squall and heavy but shortlived rain.

A cold front is drawn on a weather map either as a blue line or as a black line with jagged teeth on the side of advance. It can be seen clearly as a white curve of cloud on satellite pictures, and is often drawn as clearly in the sky to observers on the ground. The change from pelting rain to blue sky with some convection clouds can be quite dramatic.

A cold front poses all the problems for aviators that individual cunimb make, extreme wind shear in squalls, aqua planing conditions on the runway, sometimes hail. One possible redeeming feature is that a cold front can be tracked and timed approximately, whereas individual cunimb are small random features in the weather scene which cannot be pinpointed until near arrival.

A cold front disappearing in the distance, after giving a short-lived but torrential downpour.

In the vertical plane, the boundary between cold air and warm slopes slightly backward from the ground.
A warm front is the ground level boundary between warm air and cooler air downwind, over which it is being forced to ascend by the pursuing cold front. The boundary between the warm and cool air in the vertical plane is a comparatively shallow slope, with lift being less violent but more persistent than lift at the cold front. Clouds heralding a warm front appear several hundred miles downwind, visible simply because of their elevation in the sky.

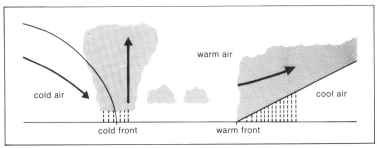

Vertical cross section through a cold and warm front. Cirrus, cloud first visible 300-500 miles ahead of warm front.

First appear feathery wisps of ice crystal cloud, called *cirrus*, several miles high. Gradually these blend into a continuous veil of *cirrostratus*, which dims the Sun enough to curtail thermal activity below. Cloud lowers and thickens to a formless grey waterdrop cloud called *altostratus* as the warm front advances, giving rain or snow soon after the Sun is completely obscured. Rain may be light or heavy according to the vigour of the front, but it usually lasts for several hours, during which time low

Small cumulus below, except over the Thames estuary. Cirrus and altostratus in distance.

Small cumulus below, and lenticular alongside, from an aircraft flying roughly at rightangles to the wind. *M. J. Hammersley*

Dust devil, near Phoenix, Arizona. *S. B. Idso*

Cirrus tufts consolidating into a film of cirrostratus and thickening on the horizon to altostratus, indicating approach of warm front
M. J. Hammersley

Altrostratus blurring the Sun and darkening towards the horizon — rain very soon.

cloud called *nimbostratus* forms in the turbulent moist air near the ground. It may be only a few hundred feet above ground and often shrouds high ground as hill fog.

A warm front, like a cold front and the depressions with which they are usually associated, travels by day or night and at any season. On weather charts a warm front is shown by a red line, or a black line with semicircles on the side of advance.

A halo round the moon indicates ice crystal cloud ahead of a warm front. Colours are red on the inside and yellow and blue outside, though sometimes the colours are so faint that the halo looks whitish. (A corona, sometimes seen through thin water drop cloud, is bluish on the inside and red-brown outside; this has no significance for predicting a warm front.)

Freezing rain, causing *glazed frost*, occurs when a cold winter spell is about to collapse because of an advancing warm front. Rain ahead of the front falls through the sub-freezing air below

Grasses weighed down by glazed frost, formed by freezing rain.
M. J. Hammersley

and creates ice over everything it touches. The condition usually only lasts a few hours, until the warm front arrives and temperatures rise.

The warm sector air, behind the warm front features little high or medium level cloud. During the day in summer small fair weather cumulus develop, clearing at night; in winter both day and night, low stratus cloud is more likely as warm moist air cools in the colder latitudes.

An occlusion is the surface boundary between air behind a cold front and the air ahead of a warm front. This happens because a cold front travels faster than a warm front, eventually overtaking it and lifting the warm sector air right off the ground. The cloud sequences remain the same as for two separate fronts, but compressed so that there is no warm sector intermission at ground level.

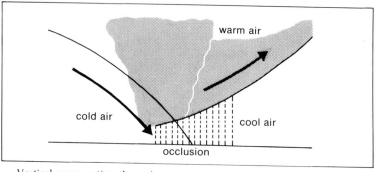

Vertical cross section through an occlusion

An occlusion usually indicates that the original warm and cold fronts are a few days old so that their distinctive boundaries are becoming mixed and blurred. The occlusion may disperse into patchy altostratus without rain, or may be resurrected into vigorous activity by any new infusion of air around the associated low pressure system.

Wind directions change at the passage of fronts, often abruptly at low level. The sharp angle between isobars either side of fronts shown on weather charts reflects reality, not some whim of the draughtsman. In the Northern Hemisphere, wind at 2000 ft backs ahead of a warm front, veers as the warm front passes and then veers again at the passage of the cold front. In the Southern Hemisphere the manner of change is reversed; wind veers ahead of the warm front, and then backs again at the passage of both the warm and cold fronts.

Winds change at upper levels too, but less markedly because the pressure patterns are less pronounced and winds gradually become more westerly. When climbing near fronts in the Northern Hemisphere pilots can expect wind to veer with height ahead of the warm front, alter little with height above the warm sector and back with height behind the cold front. Again the opposite in the southern hemisphere, where wind backs with height ahead of the warm front, and veers with height behind the cold.

Typical active depressions with associated fronts

Northern hemisphere

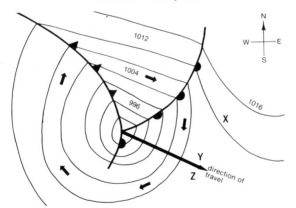

South of the centre, the wind *backs* from the direction it was blowing in the previous ridge of high pressure, as the depression and warm front advance; *veers* as the warm front passes; *veers* again, usually very noticeably, as the cold front passes.

North of the centre, the wind *backs all the time* that the depression advances and moves across an area, until the wind eventually becomes the same, in the rear of the depression, as that experienced by someone who was south of the centre.

Southern hemisphere

North of the centre, wind *veers* from the direction it was blowing in the previous ridge of high pressure, as the depression and warm front advance; *backs* as the warm front passes; *backs* again, usually very noticeably, as the cold front passes.

South of the centre, the wind *veers all the time* that the depression advances and moves across an area, until the wind eventually becomes the same, in the rear of the depression, as that experienced by someone who was north of the centre.

A trough of low pressure is an elongated extension of the isobars from the centre of a depression, often from one which has become slowmoving, even stationary. All trace of the original fronts may be lost, but there is nevertheless convergence in towards the trough from either side, lifting air, replenishing the circulation with air from quite different directions and creating cloud and rain. Sometimes this can last for days on end because the depression has no forward movement and the convergence is a continuing rain factory which results in floods.

A secondary depression often forms on a trailing and dying front which becomes rejuvenated by fresh incursions of contrasting airs. A secondary can often be more vicious than the original depression and can brew gale winds very quickly. In the British Isles, secondaries often develop in the south west approaches, and journey up the English Channel where funnelling increases the risk of gales.

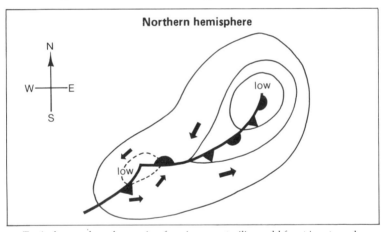

Typical secondary depression forming on a trailing cold front in a trough.

Lee depressions sometimes form when a fresh wind blows across a mountain range which acts as a barrier to the free flow of air. The low pressure area to leeward is usually a small scale and temporary circulation but occasionally grows to become a vigorous depression with fronts.

Thermal lows form in fine weather when sea breezes converge from different angles across complicated coast lines. These lows may trigger cloud, even rain, when other areas have none.

Polar lows occur in winter when very cold air blows into latitudes where the sea is much warmer. Though the thermal stimulus is not as great as it can be over land in summer, it is

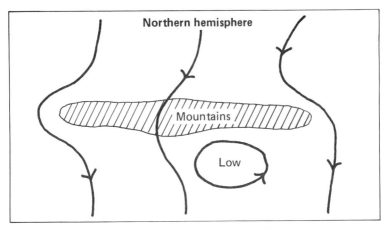

A lee depression sometimes forms when wind is deflected by a mountain range.

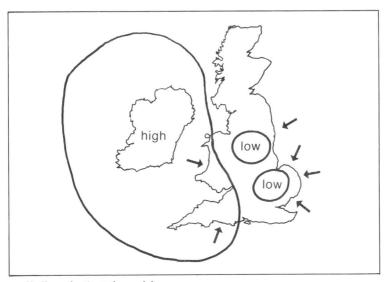

Shallow daytime thermal lows

made specially effective because the upper air is so cold and the atmosphere unstable. Polar lows can brew up quite nasty weather and once formed may feature on the weather chart for some days.

Tropical storms are the most violent of low pressure systems, and were familiar to sailors long before the connection between pressure and wind was fully understood. Sailors described the circular wall of towering clouds around the cloudless and

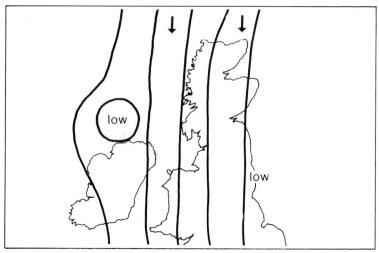

Polar low

relatively calm eye, and the manner in which the winds circulated in either hemisphere. These storms originate over tropical seas where there is an abundance of warm air and moisture, travel westwards at first before recurving towards the east into middle latitudes. Wind speeds tend to decrease when these storms cross on to land, but precipitation may get even worse because of extra lift over high ground. The storms eventually degenerate to depressions and die out.

The storms were originally given the name *cyclone* because of their circulating winds. Today the term *tropical cyclone* is reserved for low pressure circulations having wind speeds greater than force 8 but less than force 12. Force 12, with average wind speeds of more than 64 kts, earns a storm the name of *hurricane,* or *typhoon* if in the Pacific.

Food for thought
What happens when winds of different temperature converge?
What is a trough of low pressure?
What is the sea breeze front?
Is there any diurnal rhythm to cold and warm fronts?
How would landing conditions be affected by the passage of a cold front?
What cloud base would you expect with the passage of a warm front?
How would you first notice the approach of a warm front, by day, by night?
How do winds at 2000 ft change with the passage of a depression and fronts?

Infra red view from NOAA5 of eastern Atlantic and Europe at 8.00 pm on 9 October 1976, just after the UK heat wave had broken and fine weather retreated to the Mediterranean. Families of depressions affected the British Isles with associated warm and cold fronts. Coldest temperatures, ie, highest clouds are the whitest. Picture taken at 2000 hrs, by which time Italy was cooler than the sea, therefore lighter grey, while snow over the Alps appears whiter still. Note the dark coloured rivers running down from the Alps. *Courtesy of Dundee University.*

11 Diverging winds and subsidence, with high pressure

Anticyclone is the name given to a high pressure circulation because it is so different, indeed opposite, to a cyclone. Isobars around the centre are usually widely spaced indicating light wind, although there may be strong winds on the outer

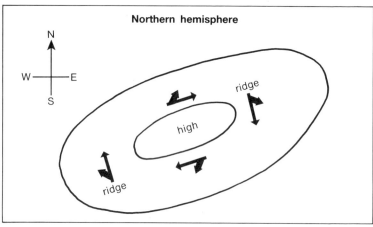

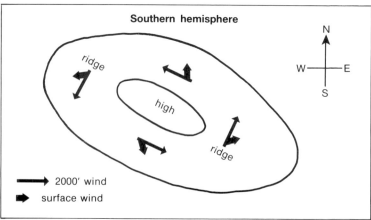

Typical anticyclone. High pressure pattern with wind blowing clockwise in the northern hemisphere and anticlockwise in the southern.

boundaries if the anticyclone is resisting the advance of a depression. High pressure systems drift, rather than travel with measurable speed and they produce sluggish rather than vigorous weather. Cells of high pressure girdle the Earth in the subtropics and are frequent over the Poles. High pressure also develops over large continents in winter when there is intense cooling of land and increasingly dense air. Ridges of high pressure often extend from either direction to the temperate regions, but only occasionally do they become fully established anticyclones, after a slow persistent rise in pressure.

Subsidence of air is the key to anticyclonic weather. Wind near the ground diverges from the centre, in both hemispheres, upper air subsides to replace the net outflow of air below and in consequence warms because of compression under greater atmospheric pressure. Higher temperature means increased capacity for water vapour, and evaporation nibbles away at the top of cumulus clouds, which become blurred. In the first day or two of high pressure, cumulus bases remain firm looking, but the clouds become shallower each day until the sky remains cloudless, however hot the Sun. In summer the result is a heat wave; in winter, one clear fine day leads either to hard frost at night if the air mass is dry or to fog if the air is moist.

A heat wave in summer produces only shallow dry thermals, without any cumulus clouds to mark their presence. Glider pilots must watch the birds or study the composition of the ground below for clues to the rising air currents.

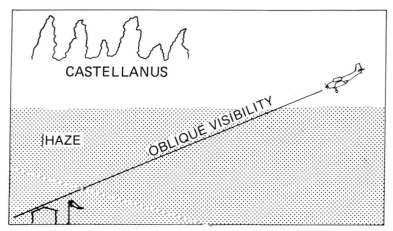

In high pressure, stable air keeps haze trapped near the ground, giving poor oblique visibility. In summer, hot air may eventually break through to an upper unstable layer of air, where castellanus clouds and thunderstorms develop.

Cumulus castellanus over mountains shooting upwards in a manner indicating very unstable air. Probable thunderstorms by evening.

While subsiding air above the anticyclone creates a very stable lower atmosphere, the upper air becomes unstable, because the layers near the tropopause are supplied by colder air from all sides. Eventually, hot air from the lower stable levels breaks through into the unstable atmosphere above, where tall turrets of convection cloud, called *castellanus*, build up rapidly. Their bases are often shrouded in haze but the tops loom up through the dark grey-purple cloud, often higher than 8000 ft above ground. A propensity to headaches and the clammy moist atmosphere together with the threatening cloud foretells thunderstorms.

High level thunderstorms have a short life but each propagates another in the vigorous see-sawing of air in the unstable upper atmosphere. Upper winds are usually light, so that storms continue sometimes all night, appearing to roll around in a circle. These storms often reach southern England on southeasterly winds from France, when low pressure may break up the anticyclone altogether or merely be a brief interlude before resumption of fine weather.

A winter anticyclone produces weather dependent upon the humidity of the air mass. If high pressure builds up within dry air, one fine day will be followed by a cold night and yet another fine day. However, because of the long hours of cooling at night and the low altitude of the Sun by day, air temperatures get progressively colder as the anticyclone persists. All the lowest temperatures are recorded in this kind of still, anticyclonic weather, and the ground gets rock hard with frost.

In damp air, however, for instance coming from the subtropical high pressure belt towards the British Isles across the Atlantic, even one night with cloudless skies may permit air to cool to dew point or below. Fog forms, quickest near moist places like rivers and lakes, and in hollows to which cold air drains. It may form too over the sea if that is near its spring minimum temperature. If the wind is more than about 10 knots condensation can be lifted off the ground as low cloud, called stratus, cloaking the country in well-named anticyclonic gloom. That at any rate maintains reasonable visibility for land and sea traffic, but can be very dicey for aircraft landing.

Neither fog nor stratus clear in winter until there is a radical change in wind direction or pressure system. Fog forms most easily when there are plenty of nucleii on which condensation can occur. The smog of 1952, between 5 and 9 December, was the modern equivalent of the Victorian peasoupers. There was an easterly drift of air across London from the industrial areas of which the most lethal component was sulphur dioxide, which combined with water drops to give sulphuric acid. Deaths during the period were more than 7 times greater than usual mainly amongst the old and the ill. No smogs have occurred in Great Britain since the Clean Air Act of 1956.

Smoke held down beneath a temperature inversion over Christchurch, New Zealand. *M. J. Hammersley*

Visibility is always poor in anticyclones. It starts to deteriorate once a ridge of high pressure causes subsidence of air aloft, and gets steadily worse as the ridge developes into an anticyclone. Dirt in the lower atmosphere remains trapped below an inversion of temperature, making the sky merely whitish-blue instead of the deep clear blue of unstable air. Downwind of industrial areas the sky may look ominous enough to make one fear a storm, but in winter at any rate there is unlikely to be rain — just so much dirt in the air that electric lights are needed by early afternoon.

Oblique visibility from air to ground is always worse than horizontal visibility along the runway, because of the thickness of atmosphere through which one must see.

Food for thought
What barometric tendency would herald an anticyclone?
What is the consequence of diverging winds near the ground?
What are castellanus clouds, and how do they differ from cumulus formed in thermals rising from the ground?
What night time weather can you expect in winter from an anticyclone having moist air, dry air?
How does visibility in an anticyclone compare with that in unstable air behind a depression?

12 Tricks of the Light

Light can play peculiar tricks in various weather conditions, and some can be unnerving unless one knows they can happen.

Light travels in straight lines within a homogeneous medium, though the 'lines' are in fact wave motion of very short wavelength and amplitude. Light can bend *(diffraction)* around particles or water drops having approximately the same radius as the wave length of light, and can even be *scattered* by the molecules of air itself. But white light consists of many colours, which are diverted by different amounts. In a clean sky only the shortest wave band, blue, is scattered and the sky appears blue, with the Sun remaining yellow or whitish. In a dirty or moist atmosphere, where light from most wave bands is scattered, the Sun appears red and the sky whitish. Occasionally, as the Sun's rim appears or disappears on the horizon a momentary green flash appears when the atmosphere is clean and dry. A pilot once reported in the journal 'Weather' having seen the greenflash twice on descent towards a false horizon of altostratus. After 5 seconds, the first green flash disappeared for 2 seconds, and then reappeared for a further 3 seconds, probably because his aircraft was descending at about the same rate as the Sun was rising.

As for clouds, scattering and multiple reflections from a dense mass of water drops makes them look brilliantly white when in direct sunlight, grey when shaded and often unnecessarily threatening and black when lit from behind by a low Sun. Flying within cloud is just confusing whiteness, with no texture or colour contrast to help the brain interpret what the eye sees. Similar whiteouts occur below low cloud when the ground is completely covered in snow. Reflections up and down from both blot out the horizon and every contour shadow, disorientating the mind. Paradoxically, travellers over polar landscapes often navigate by the different reflections thrown up on to low cloud from the varied surfaces below. *Ice blink* is the glare from ice and a *water sky* the grey map of reflections projected upwards from open water.

Light passing from one transparent medium to another bends *(refracts)* so that a straight stick in a bucket of water appears

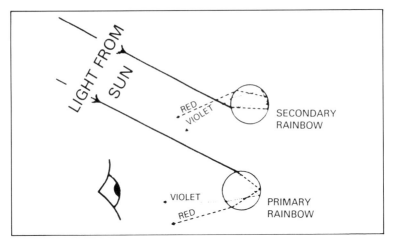

Light is refracted through water drops, and reflected from the back surface; once, to give a primary rainbow, twice to give a secondary bow with reversed colours.

angled. When light is refracted twice in the same direction, through a prism or water drop, it may emerge split into the colours of the spectrum. Light may also be reflected off the back surface of water drops, as well as being refracted on the passage through, so that emerging light almost back-tracks along the way it entered the drop. Hence the rainbow, seen by anyone facing a screen of large water drops falling as rain, from a waterfall or even spray from a wet road, with the Sun directly behind. The only colours returning to the eye are those from drops on the segment of a circle whose centre is the antisolar point, an imaginary shadow of the eye in the distance. That means a point on the ground for those without wings, but can be within the screen of drops for a pilot approaching in the air, who may be privileged to see a full circle. Of course, it is impossible to reach the end of a rainbow, because as soon as you move so does the antisolar point and the rainbow itself. Every circular optical phenomenon is unique to the one person viewing it, and slightly different from that seen by someone alongside. Rainbows are typical of showery weather when there is both sunshine and rain within view, and they are only visible when the Sun's altitude is between 42° and 53°.

Fog and cloud contain smaller water drops than rain, which do not give good colour separation. So a fog bow, seen between sun and fog lifting out of a valley, for instance, is bright but white. Theoretically a pilot approaching a cloud lit by the Sun should see a cloud bow, but in practice the intense reflections and scattering renders the bow invisible. Looking down on to fog from high ground or from an aircraft one may see a circular glory of light around the shadow of one's head or the aircraft, which may have a reddish tinge of colour on the outside.

When you see the moon *through* a sheet of thin water drop cloud (low stratus or stratocumulus) it may be encircled by one or more corona, having pale colours, red on the outside, blue inside like a glory. This has no particular forecasting significance, unlike a halo which has an opposite colour sequence — red inside and blue outside. Haloes form when light is refracted though thin ice crystal cloud (cirrus) which is often the first warning of the approach of a warm front. Haloes also form around the Sun when that is thinly veiled by cirrus, but these are less visible because of general daylight. On no account try to study a daytime halo without blotting out the Sun itself with some solid object before the eyes.

Occasionally quite extraordinary geometric patterns embellish the basic circular halo, according to the type of ice crystals in the cloud — prisms or columns or plates, aligned vertically or horizontally, regularly or at random. Mock suns, tangent arcs, circumzenithal arcs, sun pillars, even fiery crosses — there seems no end to the ingenuity of display in the sky. You, too, may see something no one else has witnessed before, so remember to sketch or photograph it.

Apart from water drops and ice crystals, weather processes produce some drastic changes in density within adjacent layers

Part of a halo display seen at Saskatoon, Canada on 3 December 1970. W. J. *Evans*

of air. Travellers in the desert have often been tortured by inverted images in the distance which seem to be bordering life-giving pools of water. The same happens over a hot tarmac road as you approach the brow of a hill — it momentary dissolves into a wobbly, watery skyline which can be quite disconcerting, because you know the road can't really disappear. These are *inferior mirages,* the image of the sky shimmering like water in the superheated layer of air close to the ground. The light from the distant scene bends upwards towards the eye as it is refracted through the less dense hot air, but the image which the eye sees appears along a straight line from the eye. Likewise, a *superior mirage* upright may appear in the sky, the image of something which may be below the horizon, simply because the air near the ground is exceptionally cold and dense. In polar regions, the Sun often sets and then reappears again to reach the eye from below the horizon, setting yet again some minutes later. On May 26, 1978 Hull docks in north Humberside were clearly seen on the skyline from Bridlington 25 miles away, so sharply that even the cranes could be seen working.

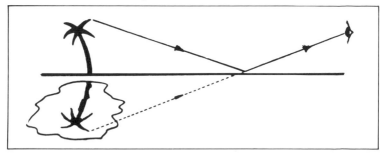

Inferior mirage, inverted, seen when light is refracted upwards towards the eye through hot, shimmering air.

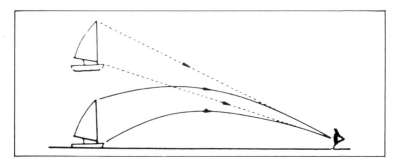

Superior mirage, upright, seen above the real object when light is bent downwards through layers of cold air.

A superior mirage of the Edwards Air Force Rocket Test Site in the Mojave Desert, South California, viewed, appropriately, from El Mirage about 20 miles further south. Photographs taken with a 35 mm Nikon camera, with 450 mm lens attached, at 8.03 am on 12.26.80 when air temperature was 5°C. *G. Uveges*

The distant images were constantly changing but were all gone by 9.12 am when the air temperature had risen to 10.5°C. *G. Uveges*

13 Weather forecasting

It is not too difficult to understand how any particular aspect of the weather happens, but it is quite a different problem to forecast a combination of features for one or several days ahead. The huge demand for weather information by aviators in the Second World War and in the later expansion of commercial aviation, led to technological miracles to help meteorologists. Nevertheless, the final words of wisdom still come from human beings, surrounded by computer plotted charts and readouts, and satellite pictures of clouds. Pilots should have some idea of how it's all put together, both to understand the messages and also the limits of accuracy involved.

Satellites have extended human eyesight so that we can see clouds all over the world, by pictures taken on visible wavelength during the daytime and also by images taken on infra-red which are as clear at night as by day. In these, the coldest clouds, land or sea appear the whitest and the warmer features look grey through to black. In addition satellites have sensors which can record temperature and humidity of the atmosphere below, and will undoubtedly be able to perform still more clever observations in the future.

A sunsynchronous satellite passes over an area at approximately the same local time every day, over-riding each Pole every two hours and covering the entire Equator twice a day. As it travels, the Earth rotates beneath, so that places between Equator and Poles are viewed from different angles in three consecutive passes twice every 24 hours. These satellites cruise about 500 miles above the Earth.

Geosynchronous satellites cruise at 22,300 miles above the Earth, so as to remain stationary relative to the Equator below. Instruments scan the Earth, strip by strip in sequence, so that after correction for time lag a circular picture of the half globe below is obtained. That takes about half an hour, and the process begins all over again, to give the forecaster an invaluable time lapse sequence of what is going on. The edges of these pictures are too distorted to be useful but there are 5 geosynchronous satellites around the world which, together

Infra-red picture from NOAA5 (sunsynchronous) taken during the August heat wave of 1976. Land black (because warmest surface); light grey currents in Irish Sea and Channel (colder than Atlantic); white area over North Sea high cloud from front over Scandinavia.
Courtesy of Dundee University

View of the half world from Meteosat on 7 July 1979 on visible wave length. Note depression approaching Spain. *Courtesy of Dundee University.*

with the sunsynchronous satellites, give reasonable coverage everywhere.

However, satellite data comprises present facts; cloud patterns do not travel without at the same time changing; and time lapse sequences are hindcasting rather than forecasting. Sometimes weather systems advance in uncomplicated fashion, so that one can extrapolate from what *was* to what *will be*, but many times they decide to 'do their own thing', apparently by whim. Satellites are very superior observers, but they are not forecasters.

Computers are able to process complicated thermodynamic equations in minutes but of course they can only give answers when they are fed facts. The atmosphere is so vast that it is only possible to collect a sample of pertinent facts from the infinite total. Some criteria even have to be estimated from known data elsewhere in order to build a symmetrical computer model of the atmosphere. Nevertheless, forecast pressure charts for a few days ahead have proved more reliable when made by computer than by forecaster, and are now used all the time. They are corrected, should actual events prove contrary to expectations, before being projected into the next forecast period. Computers can also produce general forecasts for cloud, wind, temperature and rainfall, although the detail needed by the public is always likely to be arrived at by a human brain reasoning around evidence and drawing upon a fund of past experience.

So, computers can forecast but they are more accurate for a short period ahead than for a long. At the moment, three days ahead is a fairly reliable forecast period, and between four and ten days the computer makes a brave attempt but 'could do better'. It is unlikely that computers can ever take over all forecasting, though some people with more faith may think differently.

Facsimile machines serve forecasters very well these days, and also transmit weather information to airfields which cannot justify the presence of a forecaster. The machines disgorge already plotted weather charts, predicted pressure patterns and upper air charts, and satellite pictures. Teleprinters chatter incessantly with the latest weather observations, grouped together by area and transmitted in numerical code.

Synoptic weather observations are descriptions of weather at different places at the same hour, which are summarised into numerical code for ease of transmission as rapidly as possible. The code is agreed within the World Meteorological Organisation (WMO), a model of international co-operation in a rather aggressive world, so that one can be sure that all weather offices are working upon the same basic data.

There are some 5000 weather stations within the WMO, making observations every hour of night and day, as well as about 1000 stations which collect upper air data by radio sonde. Electronic instruments monitor many inaccessible areas and commercial shipping and airlines report back on weather encountered. Everything is fed into an international telecommunications network and then processed by regional headquarters before being fed back to outstations. A meteorologist can easily decipher each line of numerical code which is received, but whole sheets of figures do not make immediate sense in terms of what weather is happening where. So the coded messages are translated into symbols and plotted in special positions around station circles on a map, giving a picture of weather.

The symbol code is very detailed, 99 items for weather alone, 40 for cloud type and 10 ways of filling the station circle to show

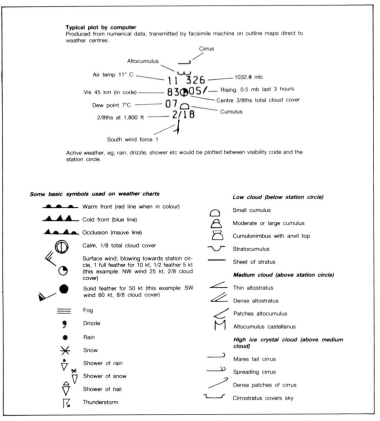

Typical plot by computer
Produced from numerical data, transmitted by facsimile machine on outline maps direct to weather centres.

Cirrus
Altocumulus
Air temp 11° C — 11 326 — 1032.8 mb
Vis 45 km (in code) — 83005/ — Rising. 0.5 mb last 3 hours
Dew point 7°C — 07 — Centre 3/8ths total cloud cover
2/8ths at 1,800 ft — 2/18 — Cumulus
South wind force 1

Active weather, eg, rain, drizzle, shower etc would be plotted between visibility code and the station circle.

Some basic symbols used on weather charts

Warm front (red line when in colour)
Cold front (blue line)
Occlusion (mauve line)
Calm, 1/8 total cloud cover
Surface wind, blowing towards station circle, 1 full feather for 10 kt, 1/2 feather 5 kt (this example: NW wind 25 kt, 2/8 cloud cover)
Solid feather for 50 kt (this example: SW wind 60 kt, 8/8 cloud cover)
Fog
Drizzle
Rain
Snow
Shower of rain
Shower of snow
Shower of hail
Thunderstorm

Low cloud (below station circle)

Small cumulus
Moderate or large cumulus
Cumulonimbus with anvil top
Stratocumulus
Sheet of stratus

Medium cloud (above station circle)

Thin altostratus
Dense altostratus
Patches altocumulus
Altocumulus castellanus

High ice crystal cloud (above medium cloud)

Mares tail cirrus
Spreading cirrus
Dense patches of cirrus
Cirrostratus covers sky

Sample weather plot and symbols, as used on synoptic charts.

total cloud amount. Pilots should know enough to be able to see what is pertinent, weatherwise; lots of black dots mean a rainy day, stars indicate snow, and spiky triangles are showers. The more feathers on the surface wind vanes, all blowing in towards the station circle, the windier the day. It should be sufficient to recognise 10 basic descriptions of cloud, classified according to shape (rounded or flat) and minimum height of base. Latin terms are used;- *cirrus* (hairlike) for ice crystal clouds above about 16,500 ft, and *alto* (medium level) for clouds with base above 6500 ft. Cumulus means rounded at any level and *stratus* means flat, while anything giving rain or snow adds the term *nimbus*. Symbols mirror these terms with curves and straight lines, and simple abbreviations appear on briefing charts. **The computer plotted weather chart is completed** by the forecaster himself, who will already have some idea of what to expect from the sequence of past charts.

He pinpoints the centres of high and low pressure by the extreme values reported and by the way the surface winds are circulating. The fronts are drawn between places which have tell-tale differences in weather.

Ahead of a warm front — rain or snow, falling pressure, an overcast sky.

Behind a warm front — rain ceased and reported as past weather, pressure steadied, wind veered (in Northern Hemisphere), broken cloud. Dew point higher in the new air mass, a more telling factor than temperature, which can change simply because of the position of the Sun.

Immediately ahead of a cold front — heavy rain, overcast sky

Behind a cold front — rain ceased and reported as past weather, veered wind, rising pressure, lower dew point.

Well broken sky with cumulus or cunimb.

If these symptoms are not immediately obvious, it probably means that the fronts are dying out and the differences between the air masses becoming less pronounced because of mixing. The forecaster then draws the isobars, starting with any two equal values, joining the stations lightly in pencil. Since the isobars represent the wind direction at 2000 ft they will be slightly veered from the surface winds reported (in the Northern Hemisphere). Portions of isobars are then drawn

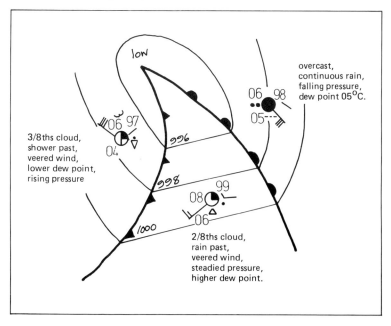

through other pressure values, interpolated where necessary and spaced according to reported wind strengths. Gradually the whole map is covered by isobars, and experienced forecasters can complete the smooth flowing patterns at great speed. Then starts the detective work.

Forecast positions of high and low pressure centres are estimated on advice from headquarters or by rule-of-thumb that depressions travel in the direction of the wind in the warm sector. Anticyclones tend to drift without purpose, and are harder to track.

All fronts are advanced according to the scales printed on the map in use, and the station reports scrutinised for any signs of diminishing activity or intensification. Rates of pressure change are significant, and pressure falls or rises of more than 8 mb in three hours is an almost certain sign of gales. But gales can also brew up with less pressure changes; there are no hard and fast rules in forecasting!

In winter, decisions have to be made about whether precipitation is likely to be rain or snow — a trifling variation in temperature several hundred feet above ground can make all the difference in marginal situations.

When there are no fronts on the map or approaching, a forecaster debates the chance of convection clouds.

Unstable deep cold air behind a depression, giving cunimb and showers?

Stable air in a temporary ridge before the next depression, with small cumulus?

Dispersal of all cumulus as an anticyclone builds up, with slow persistent rise in pressure?

How high will cumulus build?

Showers of rain or snow, with or without hail and thunder?

Any high ground to accentuate cloud development with extra lift?

What of the following night? Air mass moist so that clear skies lead to fog? Air dry, so that frost occurs in winter?

Will the Sun's strength permit fog to clear next day? If not on the basis of temperature rises expected, will there be a tiny increase in wind speed, quite unpredictable, and lift fog off the ground as stratus?

It is the nature of meteorology to be imprecise and it is the occupational hazard for the forecasters to be sometimes wrong, but never on purpose. The best forecasting results are achieved when the recipient of a professional forecast understands the subject well enough to be able to add the weather peculiarities of his own locality.

Food for thought
What do white, grey and black colours indicate in satellite pictures taken on infra-red wavelength?
How does a geosynchronous satellite orbit?
What are the international weather symbols for rain, drizzle, snow, showers?
What wind strength is indicated by one and a half feathers on a wind vane?
What wind, weather, pressure and dew point changes would indicate the passage of a cold front?
What three-hourly pressure change would make gales seem highly likely?

14 Meteorological information for aviators

Since aircraft travel faster than the weather, most aviation forecasts come within the short period ahead category, and have a better chance of accuracy than forecasts for, say, shipping crossing the Atlantic. Nevertheless, landing conditions can quickly deteriorate from the tricky to the impossible, so that concise weather information is often needed in a hurry. In the UK the Civil Aviation Authority and the Meteorological Office have devised codes which are simplified versions of the international weather code, and weather messages are transmitted frequently on the Operational Meteorogical Teleprinter Circuit (OPMET) and the Aeronautical Fixed Telecommunications Network (AFTN).

METARS are Meteorological Airfield Reports, facts about actual weather at specified stations, updated every half hour. The METAR signal is followed by the time of observation and the station code letters; and then groups of numerals and letters designating wind direction and speed, visibility, weather and two groups for cloud amounts, type and height above ground. Temperature and dew point and QNH pressure complete the messages. The code CAVOK indicates that there is no cloud below 5000 ft or significant for flight, no adverse weather and visibility is OK.

METARS and CAVOK are fact, not forecast.

TAFs are Terminal Airfield Forecasts of conditions expected at specified stations, within a nine hour period ahead, and upgraded every three hours to take account of further developments. The only substantial language difference between a METAR and a TAF is in the time group, a specific hour and minute in the METAR, but a period of time in the TAF, eg, 0615 means 0600 hours until 1500 hours.

TAFs may be followed by qualifying messages, all fairly easy to read. For instance,

TEMPO0911 2000 6ST004 means there may be a temporary change, lasting less than an hour, between the hours 0900 and 1100, with visibility down to 2000 metres and 6/8 stratus at 400 ft.

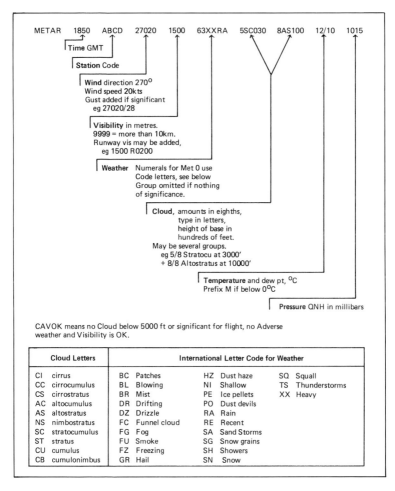

METAR 1850 ABCD 27020 1500 63XXRA 5SC030 8AS100 12/10 1015

Time GMT

Station Code

Wind direction 270°
Wind speed 20kts
Gust added if significant
    eg 27020/28

Visibility in metres.
9999 = more than 10km.
Runway vis may be added,
    eg 1500 R0200

Weather   Numerals for Met 0 use
          Code letters, see below
          Group omitted if nothing
          of significance.

Cloud, amounts in eighths,
       type in letters,
       height of base in
       hundreds of feet.
   May be several groups.
     eg 5/8 Stratocu at 3000'
       + 8/8 Altostratus at 10000'

Temperature and dew pt, °C
Prefix M if below 0°C

Pressure QNH in millibars

CAVOK means no Cloud below 5000 ft or significant for flight, no Adverse
weather and Visibility is OK.

Cloud Letters		International Letter Code for Weather					
CI	cirrus	BC	Patches	HZ	Dust haze	SQ	Squall
CC	cirrocumulus	BL	Blowing	NI	Shallow	TS	Thunderstorms
CS	cirrostratus	BR	Mist	PE	Ice pellets	XX	Heavy
AC	altocumulus	DR	Drifting	PO	Dust devils		
AS	altostratus	DZ	Drizzle	RA	Rain		
NS	nimbostratus	FC	Funnel cloud	RE	Recent		
SC	stratocumulus	FG	Fog	SA	Sand Storms		
ST	stratus	FU	Smoke	SG	Snow grains		
CU	cumulus	FZ	Freezing	SH	Showers		
CB	cumulonimbus	GR	Hail	SN	Snow		

GRADU0912 indicates some gradual change between 0900 and 1200 hrs.

RAPID1213 shows a rapid change between 1200 and 1300 hrs.

Any of these change groups may be qualified by a percentage probability group, for instance PROB 20 TEMPO 0911.... meaning there is a 20% probability of such a change happening.

AIRMET is a telephone answering service which provides recorded weather forecasts, updated every 4 hours and at other times when required. It serves a total 30 areas in the UK and north France, grouped into three principal areas, Southern England, Northern England and Wales, and Scotland with Northern Ireland. METARS and TAFS required on request are given from 8 weather centres in different parts of the country. **SIGMET** gives warnings of weather significant for flight safety on the teleprinter network.

VOLMET provides a continuous voice broadcast on VHF/RT, giving half-hourly weather reports for selected stations. They are transmitted from Cornwall, the Isle of Wight and Surrey, as well as from Great Dunfell in Cumbria, and can be received by aircraft in flight within about 200 miles of each transmitter, depending upon flight level. Weather details are given in the same numerical code as METARS and TAFs.

If there are no more communication channels with tongue-defying acronyms already in existence, then there probably soon will be! Technology never stands still, and the demands of aviation, both commercial and sporting, increase all the time. Self-briefing by facsimile machine or teleprinter is commonly available at aerodromes, and every pilot should make a point of keeping up to date with the weather information services.

Wind and weather charts to accompany written forecasts come in various styles, and can be obtained from 18 forecast stations around the country, preferably booked in advance. The significant weather charts are a judicial mix of international symbols and word abbreviations.

Flying clubs often delegate a knowledgeable instructor to serve as a link with meteorologists, in which case information may be displayed in any suitable style.

There are some chinks in the uniformity of international

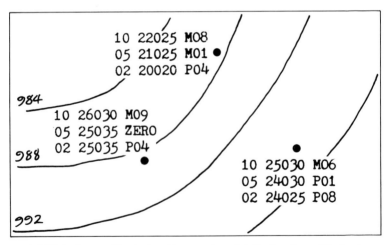

a) MSL isobars, with wind and temperature details at various altitudes in block style at specified spots. M and P indicate plus and minus, eg, M06 means minus 6°C.

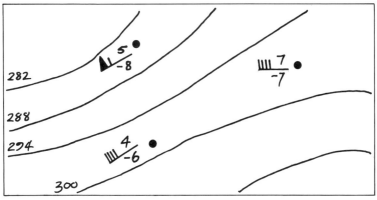

b) Contours for a specified pressure value (eg, 200 mb, 700 mb) with wind vanes. Each full feather 10 kts, each solid feather 50 kts. Shaft and feather enclose the tens figure of wind direction in degrees, eg, 5 within a vane indicating WSW means a direction of 250°. Spot temperature beneath vanes, height of each contour in decametres.

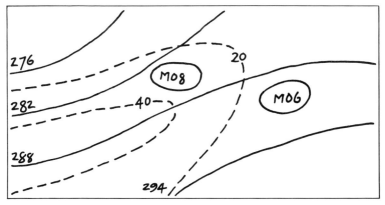

c) Contours for a specified pressure value, and spot temperatures. Pecked lines are isotachs, lines joining equal speed values (Same word derivation as *tacho*graph, installed in heavy vehicles).

units. Wind speeds are measured in knots, for the same reason that sailors have used the units for years — there are no solid milestones in the sky by which to measure distance covered in a specified time, merely celestial bodies. Everyone measures visibility in metres or kilometres, and the smaller unit of feet would give no significant additional accuracy.

However, the international code uses hundreds of feet for cloud heights and flight levels, even though meteorologists drawing upper air contour charts find decametres more practical for adequately spaced lines. Hence, charts for 700 mb,

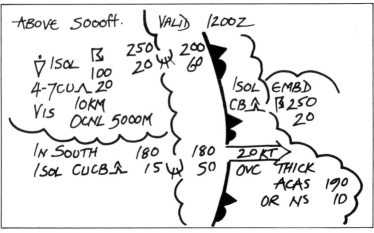

Key:

⌃ Moderate turbulence		EMBD	Embedded
⌃ Severe turbulence		OCNL	Occasional
Ⱶ Moderate icing		OVC	Overcast
ⱵⱵ Severe icing		BKN	Broken
ISOL Isolated		20KT	Speed of Front

d) Significant weather chart for specified hour, usually issued for conditions either above or below 5000 ft. Broad categories of cloud enclosed within wavy lines.

labelled for flight level 10,000 ft have contour heights measured in decametres, at intervals of 6 decametres, eg, 282, 288, 294. Take no notice, they are for professional use only. MSL charts have isobars marked in millibars, either the whole number or the last two digits, eg, 1008 or 08.

Charts for gliders, which travel more slowly than weather, usually take the form of vertical cross section through the lower atmosphere for the hours during which flying is due to take place. They are usually handwritten after consultation with a forecaster, and special symbols have evolved which are used generally all round the world.

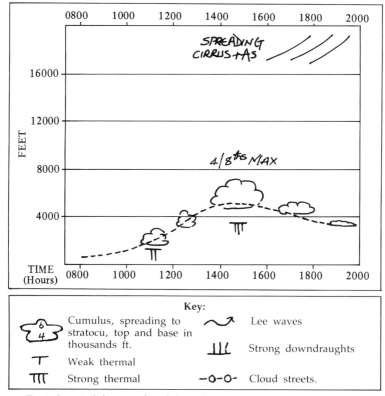

Typical period forecast for glider pilots, with appropriate symbols.

Food for thought

How do the letters R and F, in METAR and TAF, distinguish the two messages?

What is the difference in the time groups of the two messages?

What is the meaning of AS, CB, NS, RA, RE, XX?

What is VOLMET?

In what units is cloud base measured?

What wind speed is indicated by a solid feather on a wind vane?

How does a block style wind map differ from a contour map for a specific pressure level?

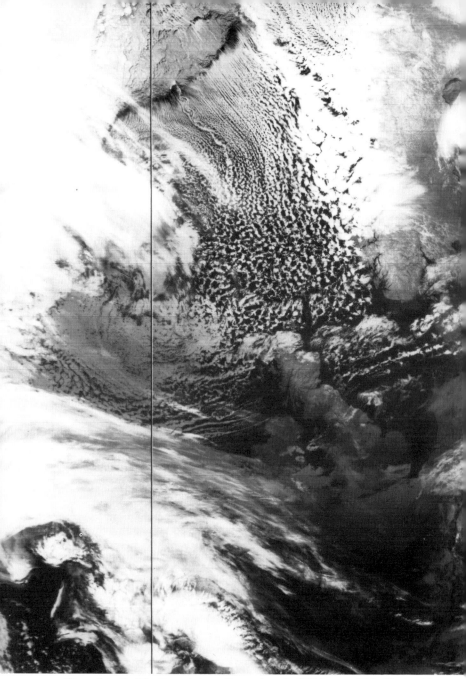

View of north Atlantic on infra-red wave length, 17 February 1978. The land is colder (therefore lighter) than the sea; cumulus clouds form over the sea as soon as cold air blows off the ice cap and get bigger as they move southwards. Two depressions approach from the west, but the British Isles are almost cloud free in a ridge of high pressure. *Courtesy of Dundee University.*

Charts
of
weather symptoms

The reminder charts overleaf, a double page for each hemisphere, summarize the information given in the rest of this book.

They relate typical skies and synoptic charts with pressure and weather sequences which may be expected to follow.

It is hoped the charts serve as a visual index to weather, just as the verbal index helps locate topics in the text of the book.

Northern hemisphere: typical weather changes consequent upon various cloud symptoms and pressure patterns.		
The sky	Cirrus increasing, cumulus tops flattening	Rainbearing altostratus and stratus covering mountain tops
General situation	Active depression moving E ▲▲▲ Warm front and ▲▲ cold front advancing with speeds measurable by geostrophic scale	Filling depression. Original fronts occluded ▲▲▲ and trailing (slack wind parallel to front gives little forward movement). **Beware sudden formation of secondary depression, often more violent than original**
Pressure pattern		
Pressure	\ Falls till warm front arrives — Steadies in warm sector / Rises sharply behind cold front	∧ Falls sharply after brief rise behind occlusion Then as in Column 1
Cloud	2 Cirrus increases to obscure sun, then // thickens to flat, grey altostratus with low - - - stratus in rain belt ◠ Small cumulus in warm sector in summer - - - Stratus in warm sector in winter ⌂ Cumulonimbus along cold front, clearing dramatically behind front	2 As in Column 1 // - - - ◠ - - - ⌂
Wind	South of centre ⤴ backing till warm front arrives ⤵ veering behind warm front ⤵ veering again behind cold front North of centre ⤴ backing all the time **Attention for gale warnings if pressure falling fast**	Changing according to position relative to new centre **Attention for gale warnings**
Weather	• Cloudy, leading to rain , Cloudy with drizzle in warm sector in winter ▽⩘ Thundery showers and squalls at cold front, becoming fair behind cold front	• As in Column 1 , ▽⩘

Cumulonimbus	Fair weather cumulus	Fog
Old depression, centre almost stationary, original fronts dissipated. **Beware sudden formation of troughs even if not indicated on previous charts**	Ridge of high pressure behind cold front, often only a temporary sandwich between one low pressure system and next	Anticyclone or high pressure area. Little pressure gradient over whole chart
low — trough	ridge — high	high
∖ Slight fall ahead of troughs ∕ Slight rise behind troughs	∕ Rises sharply behind cold front ∖ Steadies and falls if another depression advancing	— Slow, steady rise
⌂ Cumulonimbus, in unbroken line along troughs	⌂ Large cumulus at first ◠ Decreasing to small cumulus ⌒ Cirrus increasing if another front advancing	Cumulus gradually dispersing, becoming cloudless Occasional thin stratus at night, dispersing in morning according to season. Sometimes persists on coast even in summer
Gusty with extreme changes in wind direction near cumulonimbus	↺ Backing if another front approaching	Light and variable. Sea breezes develop on summer days
▽ ▽ Frequent thundery showers, prolonged in trough lines, with squalls	▽ Occasional showers at first, dying out, becoming fair	Fine but hazy in summer ≡ Fog inland in winter

99

SOUTHERN HEMISPHERE

Southern hemisphere: typical weather changes consequent upon various cloud symptoms and pressure patterns.		
The sky	Cirrus increasing, cumulus tops flattening	Rainbearing altostratus and stratus covering mountain tops
General situation	Active depression moving E ▲▲ Warm front and ▲▲ cold front advancing with speeds measurable by geostrophic scale	Filling depression. Original fronts occluded ▲▲▲ and trailing (slack wind parallel to front gives little forward movement). **Beware sudden formation of secondary depression, often more violent than original**
Pressure pattern N W——E S		
Pressure	＼ Falls till warm front arrives — Steadies in warm sector ／ Rises sharply behind cold front	＾ Falls sharply after brief rise behind occlusion Then as in Column 1
Cloud	⊃ Cirrus increases to obscure sun, then ⫽ thickens to flat, grey altostratus with low --- stratus in rain belt ⌒ Small cumulus in warm sector in summer --- Stratus in warm sector in winter ⌂ Cumulonimbus along cold front, clearing dramatically behind front	⊃ As in Column 1 ⫽ --- ⌒ --- ⌂
Wind N W——E S	**North of centre** ↻ veering till warm front arrives ↺ backing behind warm front ↺ backing again behind cold front **South of centre** ↻ veering all the time **Attention for gale warnings if pressure falling fast**	Changing according to relative position of new centre **Attention for gale warnings**
Weather	• Cloudy, leading to rain ꞈ Cloudy with drizzle in warm sector in winter ▽⍍ Thundery showers and squalls at cold front, becoming fair behind cold front	• As in Column 1 ꞈ ▽⍍

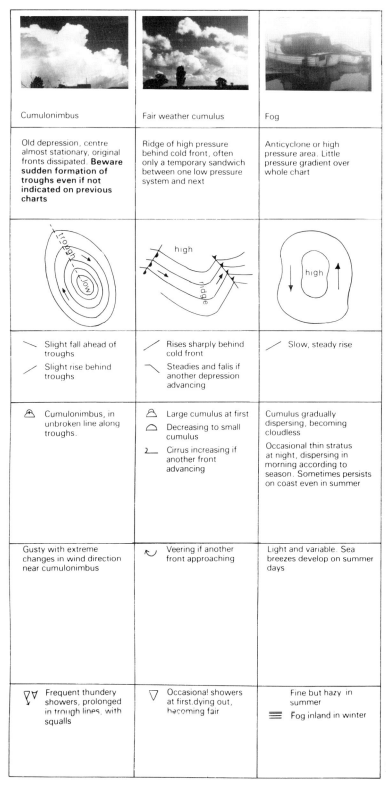		
Cumulonimbus	Fair weather cumulus	Fog
Old depression, centre almost stationary, original fronts dissipated. **Beware sudden formation of troughs even if not indicated on previous charts**	Ridge of high pressure behind cold front, often only a temporary sandwich between one low pressure system and next	Anticyclone or high pressure area. Little pressure gradient over whole chart
╲ Slight fall ahead of troughs ╱ Slight rise behind troughs	╱ Rises sharply behind cold front ╲ Steadies and falls if another depression advancing	╱ Slow, steady rise
⌂ Cumulonimbus, in unbroken line along troughs.	⌂ Large cumulus at first ⌒ Decreasing to small cumulus 2⌇ Cirrus increasing if another front advancing	Cumulus gradually dispersing, becoming cloudless Occasional thin stratus at night, dispersing in morning according to season. Sometimes persists on coast even in summer
Gusty with extreme changes in wind direction near cumulonimbus	↷ Veering if another front approaching	Light and variable. Sea breezes develop on summer days
▽▽ Frequent thundery showers, prolonged in trough lines, with squalls	▽ Occasional showers at first, dying out, becoming fair	Fine but hazy in summer ≡ Fog inland in winter

SOUTHERN HEMISPHERE

Index

Colour Pictures, between page numbers, in bold.